ARCHETYPE MODULATION THERAPY

AWAKENING THE ANIMAL WITHIN

DR P NIDHEESH

To those who were misunderstood,
not because they were wrong —
but because their energy spoke in a language
this world hadn't yet learned to hear.

To the silent Whales,
the cautious Rabbits,
the reborn Phoenixes,
and the bold Lions who had to hide their roar...

This book is for you.

And to my father,
Dr. P. Radhakrishnan,
who taught me how to see beyond symptoms
and listen to the story energy tells —
this journey began with your vision.

With gratitude,
Dr. P. Nidheesh

Contents

Contents

A Thought To Begin ....

*"Within you live many energies.
Not personalities to fix,
but archetypes to understand,
shadows to soften,
and truths to reclaim.
This book is not a mirror —
it is a doorway."*

— Dr. P. Nidheesh, MD (Hom)

FOREWORD

I began my journey in homoeopathy in 1976, when healing was not just a science — it was an act of deep listening. Over the decades, I treated patients not just through medicines, but through an understanding of their lives, their silences, and their internal battles.

In those early years, I often said:

"Every patient walks in with a symptom, but what they're really carrying is a story."

It is with that same spirit that I watched my son, Dr. P. Nidheesh, create something extraordinary.

Archetype Modulation Therapy (AMT) is not just a book. It is a lens — one that lets you see emotional struggles not as disorders, but as energy patterns looking for their right expression. Through his years of research, clinical observation, and intuition, he has brought to light what we as healers have always known — that the soul speaks in symbols.

In AMT, these symbols take the form of animal archetypes. But don't mistake them for fantasy. Each archetype here is based on repeatable clinical behaviour patterns, emotional postures, and transformation pathways I've seen mirrored in my own decades of patient care.

What impressed me most is this:
Dr. Nidheesh didn't just name energies.
He mapped how to modulate them — how to move someone from fear to courage, from chaos to clarity, from withdrawal to grounded power. And he did it without abandoning the foundation of medical rationality.

This work is the natural evolution of a healer trained in both science and symbolism. It is a bridge between what we feel and what we can transform.

To all doctors, seekers, therapists, and thinkers — this book will change the way you understand yourself, and those you serve.

And to my son:
You have not just written a book.
You have created a system that I believe will carry healing into the future.

With love and pride,
Dr. P. Radhakrishnan
Govt. Chief Medical Officer (Retd.)
Legendary Homoeopath & Mentor

Preface

This book was born from the quiet questions no diagnosis ever answered.

Why do some people break under stress, while others rebuild from it?

Why does the same symptom manifest differently in different people?

And why, in my years of clinical experience, did I keep encountering recurring emotional patterns — despite differences in age, gender, culture, or disease?

The answer came, not as a medicine, but as a metaphor.
It came as a Lion who couldn't lead without roaring,
a Rabbit who panicked in public but shone in silence,
a Phoenix who kept burning down her life just to feel reborn.

These weren't myths.
They were energies — powerful, repeatable, archetypal currents moving through my patients, my students... and myself.

And so began the journey of Archetype Modulation Therapy (AMT).
Not a theory.
A system.
A map that helps people shift from shadow to bright.
From rigidity to movement.
From personality to possibility.

This book is not about fixing you.
It's about helping you understand the energy you've been living from — and guiding you toward a more conscious, harmonious blend.

Throughout this journey, I've been blessed by the presence and wisdom of my father, Dr. P. Radhakrishnan, whose legacy of patient-centric homoeopathy shaped my entire foundation. I also acknowledge my patients, students, and readers — each of you offered a reflection that became part of this system.

This book is more than content.
It is a conversation — between your pain and your potential, your shadow and your strength.

Use it like a mirror.
Use it like a guide.
But most of all, use it like a tool for transformation.

Welcome to Archetype Modulation Therapy.
Let's begin the journey from within.

Dr. P. Nidheesh
Founder, AMT

ACKNOWLEDGEMENTS

No creation — especially one as personal and expansive as this book — is born alone. Archetype Modulation Therapy is a culmination of observation, healing, failures, revelations, and the wisdom I've had the privilege to gather from the people who walked beside me.

First and foremost, I bow with reverence to my father, Dr. P. Radhakrishnan — a legend in Indian homoeopathy, and the foundation upon which this entire work stands. Your clinical brilliance, your spiritual humility, and your unwavering integrity gave me a vision not just for medicine, but for life.

To my patients — thank you for being my greatest teachers. Each archetype in this book was first discovered not in theory, but in your stories, your struggles, and your silent strengths.

To my students and colleagues at The Homoeoschool, thank you for challenging my ideas, refining this method, and making this vision real through practice and feedback.

To the team behind my digital and therapeutic ventures — your design, editing, and technological support helped me translate a clinical truth into an accessible book.

To every healer, thinker, and rebel who believed that emotions are not weakness but wisdom — this book is for you.

And finally, to the energy that flows through us all...
May this work honour your presence.
May this system serve those who seek.
With deepest gratitude,
Dr. P. Nidheesh

Prologue

The Moment You Realised You Weren't Broken... Just Misaligned

There is a moment.

A strange, silent moment.

It doesn't always come in a breakdown.

Sometimes it comes in the middle of a perfectly good life — a job that works, a relationship that's stable, a body that doesn't complain.

And yet, something inside you whispers:

"This isn't me."

You don't know what's wrong.

You just know that you are living from the wrong energy.

Maybe you're a Rabbit trying to survive as a Tiger.

Maybe you're a Peacock told to stay invisible.

Maybe you've been burning everything down like a Phoenix, but no one ever taught you how to rise.

That whisper — the one that says "There must be more to me than this" —

it isn't your flaw.

It's your starting point.

This book is for that moment.

For the person who knows they're not broken, just... unmapped.

For the soul who's tired of personality tests that leave them feeling boxed in.

For the seeker who doesn't want labels, but a language for their energy.

Welcome to Archetype Modulation Therapy.

This isn't a system that tells you who you are.

It shows you how to move.

How to shift from fear to focus, from survival to expression, from one archetype to another — consciously, gently, powerfully.

This book is not a description of who you are.
It is an invitation to who you can become.

And it begins...
the moment you stop asking "What's wrong with me?"
and start asking

"What energy am I in right now?
And where do I want to go?"

I

The Intro..

The Animal I Was... and the One I Had to Become

I wasn't always the man who could name his inner animal.

In fact, there was a time I didn't even realise I was living through one. I thought I was just tired. Frustrated. Repeating patterns. Trying to be the best doctor, the best son, the best human being I could be.

But something always felt... off. Like I was wearing someone else's skin — like I was acting in the world but not of it.

One day, during a long moment of quiet reflection, a simple question cracked the mask I had been wearing:

"What if the traits I keep suppressing... are the parts of me I was meant to express?"

That's when I met my inner animal — not as a metaphor, but as a mirror.

And suddenly, everything began to shift.

I saw how I had been taught to roar like a Lion, while my core energy was as emotionally deep and perceptive as a Whale. I realised I was hiding my Phoenix, fearing its fire. And I'd misunderstood my Snake, seeing only the silence — not the strategy.

That day, I discovered what I now teach: That inside each of us lives an archetypal animal, waiting to be acknowledged, modulated, and expressed.

This is not about personality tests. This is not about spirit animals. This is about a therapeutic breakthrough — rooted in psychology, behavioural science, and clinical casework.

I call it Archetype Modulation Therapy (AMT). And it's changed not just my life — but the lives of hundreds who've discovered it through my clinical work, healing sessions, and teachings.

In this book, I'll guide you through:
- Discovering which animal archetype has been running your life
- Learning to modulate your traits (instead of fighting them)
- Building your blended persona — one that's confident, calm, creative, and fully YOU
- And most importantly, breaking free from the emotional cages you didn't know you were in

Because once you know your inner animal, you stop living by default — and start living by design.

Welcome to the jungle. It's time to become who you were always meant to be.

— Dr. P. Nidheesh
Founder of Archetype Modulation Therapy

PART I

The Call to Change

"This section introduces the emotional hook of AMT — identity confusion, archetypal misalignment, and the reader's awakening journey. It sets the stage for transformation by showing why most people feel "broken" when they're simply living from the wrong archetype."

II
You're Not Broken — Just Misunderstood

The Silent Struggle Behind the Smile

Most people don't fall apart with a scream.
They fall apart quietly — while still showing up on time, smiling in meetings, and answering, "I'm fine."

If that's ever been you, this chapter is for you.

I've sat across people who seemed perfectly put together. Degrees, achievements, responsibility... and still, something inside them whispered:

"Why do I feel like I'm pretending?"
"Why am I tired even when I rest?"

"Why can't I feel like myself anymore?"

And the truth is — they were not broken.
They were just misaligned with who they really are.

Take this story.

A woman in her 40s walked into my clinic one day. Smart. Respected. Quietly exhausted.
She said, "I don't even know what I want. I've just done what's needed all my life."

As I listened, I realised something:
She had been living as a Dog archetype — loyal, caring, others-first.
But every word she spoke carried the Lion's frustration — the deep, unmet need to lead, decide, and speak her truth.

She wasn't wrong for being loyal.
But she was deeply tired of living from the wrong animal.

That's where the journey begins — with a single realisation:

You are not wrong.
You are not broken.
You are just expressing the wrong archetype for who you truly are inside.

This is where AMT (Archetype Modulation Therapy) steps in.
We help you ask the most important question no one ever taught you to ask:

"Whose behaviour am I living through — and is it really mine?"

Because the answer to that question?
It will change everything.

Living from the Wrong Archetype

Have you ever felt like you're playing a role so well...
you almost forgot who you were before the performance began?

That's the feeling of living from the wrong archetype.

It's not fake.
It's not dishonest.
It's adaptive.

You had to become someone — to be liked, to stay safe, to meet expectations.

Maybe you were a bold, expressive child — full of questions and dreams.
But in school, you were scolded for being "too talkative."
So you shut your mouth and opened only your books.

Years later, you find yourself wondering why:
- You can't speak up in meetings
- You hesitate to ask for what you deserve
- You smile in groups but ache in silence

The answer is simple:
You were trained to act like a Rabbit, when your soul was

born to be a Peacock.

Or maybe you were gentle, sensitive, imaginative.
But your family celebrated toughness — not tenderness.
So you became emotionally numb, praised for being "strong."

Now, you struggle with connection.·
You keep people at a distance.
You feel safest when no one truly knows you.

You were shaped into a Snake, when you were born a Dolphin.

This is the silent wound most people carry.

They've mastered an archetype they never chose.

And here's the cost:
- Anxiety
- Exhaustion
- Emotional disconnect
- Lost identity
- A constant internal conflict between who you are and who you had to become

But here's the truth:

You're not broken.
You're not fake.
You're just tired of pretending.

AMT exists to end the pretending.

It gives you the power to:
- Name your true archetype
- Understand how and why it was buried
- And modulate your life expression — not with drama, but with awareness and ease

Because living from the wrong archetype is survival.
But modulating into your right one is freedom.

III

The Hidden Animal Within

What AMT Is

There are countless models of personality.
Enneagram. MBTI. Zodiac signs.
Each of them offers a lens — but most of them are about understanding who you are.

AMT goes further.

It's not just a system to tell you who you are.
It's a framework to help you modulate how you show up — in love, in leadership, in life.

AMT = Archetype Modulation Therapy

It's a therapeutic and transformational method that helps

you:
1. Identify your dominant emotional archetype
2. Recognise the mismatches between your internal nature and external roles
3. Learn to borrow traits from other archetypes intentionally
4. And create a blended identity that's authentic, flexible, and aligned with your goals

This isn't personality typing.
This is emotional rewiring through behaviour, awareness, and healing.

We don't ask:
"What kind of person are you?"

We ask:
"What animal is acting through you — and is it truly yours?"
"Which traits are natural, and which are survival-based?"
"How can we consciously blend animal energies to create the best version of you?"

AMT is built on three foundations:
- Archetypal Psychology (the emotional role of characters and instincts)
- Behavioural Observation (how people show their archetype through habits)
- Therapeutic Modulation (how to gently shift archetypes using daily actions and rituals)

It's not about transformation overnight.
It's about understanding the animal you've been living as —

and slowly shifting into the one your soul remembers you were meant to be.

Why We All Behave Through an Unconscious Animal Lens

You might believe you're a rational human being.
But long before you choose...
You feel.
You react.
You defend.

And those first reflexes?
They're not coming from your intellect.
They're coming from your emotional animal lens — the primal system within you that decides:
- Is this safe?
- Is this threatening?
- How do I survive this moment?

This lens isn't psychological.
It's biological.
Your nervous system doesn't read philosophy — it reads danger or safety.

And how you read the world emotionally...
is shaped by the animal pattern your brain and body have subconsciously adopted over time.

Some of us learn to fight.
Some learn to flee.
Some freeze.
Some fawn.

But all of us... adapt.

And in that adaptation, a dominant animal lens gets installed — one that starts filtering how we:
- Trust or distrust
- Connect or withdraw
- Show power or hide behind silence
- Chase dreams or sabotage them

The Animal Behind Your Reflexes

Imagine this:
- You flinch when someone raises their voice → Rabbit
- You feel anxious if you're not in control → Lion
- You joke in tension but avoid truth → Monkey / Butterfly
- You say nothing but remember everything → Snake

These are not random.
They are the default survival patterns of your inner archetype.

This is why we say in AMT:
"You don't behave as yourself.
You behave as the animal you were emotionally trained to become."

Once you see that truth, you no longer take your reactions personally.
You learn to trace them — and then... modulate them.

Because you're not your reflexes.
You're the one watching them — and you're ready now to redirect them.

How Animals Became Your Emotional Blueprint

You were born with a body, a breath, and a blank canvas.
But very quickly, life began to draw on it.

The way your parents spoke to you.
The tone of the teacher when you made a mistake.
The way your needs were answered — or ignored.

Every interaction became a signal:
"This is safe. That is not."
"This will get you love. That will get you silence."
"This is who you must become... to survive."

This is how your emotional blueprint formed.

You didn't choose it — it chose you, through repetition, reaction, and reward.

Somewhere in that process, your nervous system began to copy the traits of an animal —
not metaphorically, but instinctively.

If you were raised in a home full of shouting,
you might have become a Rabbit — alert, hyper-sensitive, constantly on edge.

If you were made responsible too early,
you could have developed into a Dog — forever helping, never asking for help.

If you were praised for performance and punished for vulnerability,
you might have grown into a Lion — always leading, never resting.

You didn't plan it. You simply became it.

Emotional Blueprints Are Animal Scripts

Over time, these survival strategies solidified into identity.
What once was just "how I get through the day"... became "who I am."

And the longer you wear the role,
the harder it becomes to remember the real you behind it.

That's why so many people feel:
- Emotionally tired
- Identity-confused
- Capable, but disconnected
- Successful, but hollow

They've succeeded as the animal they never chose to become.

But here's the hope:
Just because it became your emotional blueprint...
doesn't mean it has to be your permanent identity.

You can trace it. You can name it. You can modulate it.

And through AMT, that's exactly what you'll learn to do.

When a Rabbit Tried to Be a Lion

She was brilliant.
Top of her class. Everyone admired her discipline.

But when she sat across from me, her voice trembled.
Not because she was afraid of me —
but because she had forgotten what her own voice sounded like.

"I push myself to speak confidently," she said.
"I plan every word. I stand straight. I project authority. But I go home and cry."

This woman wasn't weak. She was just... tired.

Tired of being told to be bolder.
Tired of forcing strength when her soul was built on sensitivity.
Tired of pretending to be a Lion...
when she was actually a Rabbit.

The Cost of Living Through the Wrong Archetype

What happens when a Rabbit tries to roar?

She might learn the posture.
She might master the script.
But deep inside, her body never forgets what it means to tremble, feel, and flee.

The roar exhausts her.
The spotlight burns her skin.

The pressure to "lead" crushes the part of her that longs to be held, not praised.

This is not a story about being weak or timid.

This is a story about emotional mismatch.

Because even if your mind says, "I must succeed,"
your body still says, "But I'm not built for this kind of battle."

And that inner war? It shows up as:
- Burnout
- Anxiety
- Imposter syndrome
- Relationship breakdown
- Identity loss

Authentic Power Comes from the Right Archetype

When this woman finally accepted her Rabbit nature — not as a flaw, but as a gift —
everything changed.

She stopped pretending to be the boldest voice in the room...
and became the deepest listener instead.

She didn't chase applause...
she created emotional safety for everyone around her.

And guess what?

That quiet confidence made her more respected — not less.

Because the goal of AMT isn't to make everyone a Lion.
It's to help you stop forcing a roar when your soul was designed to breathe gently and deeply.

PART II

Meet Your Animals

"Each chapter in this part explores one or more archetypes, showcasing real-life expressions, emotional struggles, healthy vs shadow dynamics, and self-recognition tools. This is the core emotional journey of the book."

IV
The Lion – The Leadership That Heals or Hurts

He didn't walk into the room.

He entered — and the room shifted.

People listened. Paused. Looked to him before speaking.
And yet... beneath that confident air, I could feel something trembling inside.

He said,
"I have to hold it all together. If I fall apart, no one else will stand."

And there it was — the emotional script of the Lion archetype.

The Emotional Blueprint of the Lion

The Lion doesn't lead because they want to be seen.
They lead because something deep inside them believes:

"If I don't protect, no one else will."
"If I'm not strong, I'll be irrelevant."
"If I show weakness, I lose respect."

This archetype carries both power and pain. They are often admired... but rarely understood.

What Makes a Lion?

Dominant Traits: Decisive, bold, commanding
Emotional Core: Fear of weakness or loss of control
Also: Protective, responsible, struggles to receive care

Healthy Lion vs Shadow Lion

Healthy Lion:
- Inspires, empowers, leads without ego
- Uses power to protect
- Sets strong boundaries

Shadow Lion:
- Controls, dominates, suppresses others
- Uses power to punish
- Cannot tolerate criticism or vulnerability

How to Spot the Lion in You

- Do you feel uneasy if others are leading you?
- Do you often feel alone at the top?
- Do you find it hard to ask for help?
- Do you speak in absolutes (should, must, always)?
- Do you feel disappointed when others fall short?

Modulating the Lion

The Lion doesn't need to become soft.
They need to learn that vulnerability is not weakness — it's connection.

Daily Modulation Tips:
- Affirm: "I lead with strength and softness."
- Practice delegation
- Accept care from others
- Pause and respond, not react

Daily Affirmations for the Lion

"My worth is not in my control, but in my presence."
"I don't need to roar to be respected."
"I lead with honour, not ego."
"I can rest without losing my place."
"Power shared is power multiplied."

When to Use Lion Energy

Use when:
- Protecting others
- Taking decisive action
- Facing injustice

Avoid when:
- Connecting emotionally
- Trying to be heard in chaos
- Feeling threatened

V

The Owl and the Snake – Inner Vision vs Hidden Fear

They're not loud.

They don't fight for the spotlight.
But when they speak — people listen.
And when they stay silent — you feel it in the room.

These are the Owl and the Snake archetypes — two of the quietest, yet most emotionally complex energies in the AMT system.

The Owl – The Inner Observer

She sat across from me with calm eyes and folded hands.
"I watch everything," she said. "But I rarely speak unless it's needed."

The Owl doesn't seek attention. It seeks understanding.
It observes. Processes. Waits.
It wants to know why things happen, not just what happens.

Core Traits of the Owl:
- Introspective
- Wise, emotionally detached
- Excellent in strategy, learning, therapy, research
- Struggles to express emotions, but feels deeply

Owls see everything — but often forget to be seen.

The Snake – The Silent Strategist

The Snake is often misunderstood.
Where the Owl is open about its observation, the Snake hides its thoughts — not to deceive, but to protect.
It has learned that expression equals exposure. So it coils its truth, watching the world from a place of quiet calculation.

Core Traits of the Snake:
- Emotionally self-contained
- Highly intuitive and observant
- Plans ahead, expects betrayal
- Struggles with trust and vulnerability

Snakes don't lie — they reveal only what feels safe.

Healthy vs Shadow Expressions

Trait: Thinking

- Healthy Owl: Insightful, strategic
- Shadow Owl: Overanalyser, detached
- Healthy Snake: Intuitive, visionary
- Shadow Snake: Suspicious, paranoid

Trait: Emotion

- Healthy Owl: Calm, balanced
- Shadow Owl: Emotionally disconnected
- Healthy Snake: Controlled, wise
- Shadow Snake: Cold, numb, manipulative

Trait: Communication

- Healthy Owl: Selective, thoughtful
- Shadow Owl: Withholding, secretive
- Healthy Snake: Precise, subtle
- Shadow Snake: Cryptic, avoidant

How to Spot the Owl or Snake in You

- Do you prefer silence over unnecessary conversation?
- Do you replay past conversations mentally?
- Do you often feel "safer alone"?
- Do you feel like others don't truly know you — and that's how you want it?

Modulating the Owl & Snake

Both these archetypes are gifted in vision — but can become trapped in their own minds.

They must learn:
- To trust safe spaces for expression
- That vulnerability isn't weakness
- That wisdom is not just what you see — but what you share

Daily Modulation Tips:
- Journal one vulnerable truth daily
- Share a personal feeling with a trusted person
- Express needs without overthinking the response
- Move the body — release stagnant energy from overthinking

Daily Affirmations

Owl:
- "I speak even when it's not perfect."
- "My thoughts deserve a voice."
- "Insight is meant to be shared."

Snake:
- "I am safe even when I'm open."
- "Trust is a strength I grow, not a risk I fear."
- "I can be real and still protected."

When to Use Owl or Snake Energy

Use when:
- You need to understand a situation deeply
- You must plan, design, or analyse
- You need emotional self-control

Avoid when:
- You're building emotional intimacy
- You're stuck in overthinking
- You feel emotionally numb or overly distant

VI

The Dolphin – The Joyful Healer You Forgot You Were

She was the heart of every room.

Smiling, joking, encouraging everyone.
But beneath the sparkle in her eyes... was a tired soul.

"I feel like I have to keep everyone happy," she said.
"And when I'm alone, I don't know what to do with my own sadness."

This is the Dolphin.

The Emotional Blueprint of the Dolphin

Dolphins are natural emotional healers.
They lift others. Make people feel seen.
They connect deeply — through joy, humour, and light energy.

But what most people don't realise is this:
The Dolphin often hides its own wounds beneath its waves.

They fear bringing others down.
So they stay "up," even when they're silently drowning.

Core Traits of the Dolphin

- Empathic, expressive, emotionally vibrant
- Feels others' pain deeply and intuitively
- Uses joy, humour, and lightness to connect
- Avoids conflict, struggles with emotional boundaries
- Often loses energy by trying to "fix" others

Healthy vs Shadow Expression

Healthy Dolphin:
- Joyful, radiant, uplifting presence
- Connects with warmth & authenticity
- Heals others with intuition & laughter

Shadow Dolphin:
- Over-giver, emotionally drained
- People-pleaser, avoids confrontation
- Suppresses sadness, fakes joy

How to Spot the Dolphin in You

- Do people often say, "You always cheer me up"?
- Do you find it hard to say "no" when someone is hurting?
- Do you use humour to shift uncomfortable emotions?
- Do you feel unseen or unappreciated for your efforts?
- Do you break down emotionally... only in private?

Modulating the Dolphin

The Dolphin must learn that:
"It is not their job to keep everyone afloat."

They must practise self-nourishment before social rescue.

Daily Modulation Tips:
- Ask: "Am I helping or overextending?"
- Schedule alone-time without guilt
- Let others witness your sadness — don't always hide it
- Use your light to express truth, not escape it

Daily Affirmations

- "My joy is real when I include my pain."
- "I'm allowed to rest. I'm allowed to receive."
- "I don't need to perform to be loved."
- "I connect through truth, not just smiles."

When to Use Dolphin Energy

Use when:
- Bringing lightness to a heavy room
- Healing relationships through humour or empathy
- Opening emotional conversations with softness

Avoid when:
- You are feeling emotionally depleted
- You are avoiding conflict by "staying nice"
- You need to express your truth, not just ease others' discomfort

VII

The Cat and the Dog – Boundaries vs Belonging

She sat silently at the edge of the circle.
Calm. Composed. Unbothered by the buzzing conversation around her.

Meanwhile, on the other side of the room — he was already introducing himself, smiling, checking on others' comfort, offering tea.

One was a Cat.
The other, a Dog.

Both deeply emotional.
Both deeply misunderstood.

The Cat – The Soul That Needs Space

The Cat archetype isn't emotionally cold — it's self-protective.

It needs silence to breathe.
It processes emotion internally.
It bonds slowly — and only with people who honour their boundaries.

"I don't hate people. I just don't need them around all the time," one Cat-type told me.

They're often seen as distant, moody, or withdrawn.
But in truth, the Cat is teaching us this:
"Closeness without consent is invasion."

Core Traits of the Cat

- Self-contained, independent, quietly observant
- Needs solitude to regulate emotions
- Forms deep bonds but only over time
- Feels emotionally drained by constant contact
- Highly sensitive to emotional manipulation

The Dog – The Soul That Needs Connection

Dogs love deeply — and openly.

They are loyal, emotionally present, and thrive in relationships, routines, and shared purpose.

They offer themselves with sincerity and warmth.
But here's the truth many Dogs carry silently:
"I give to everyone... and sometimes forget to give to myself."

Core Traits of the Dog

- Affectionate, loyal, emotionally attuned
- Seeks belonging and closeness
- Feels responsible for others' happiness
- Struggles when unacknowledged or rejected
- Can become overly dependent or lose self in relationships

Healthy vs Shadow Expression

Trait: Emotional Style

- Healthy Cat: Clear boundaries, self-trust
- Shadow Cat: Emotionally withdrawn, avoidant
- Healthy Dog: Loving, loyal, supportive
- Shadow Dog: Clingy, self-sacrificing, needy

Trait: Energy

- Healthy Cat: Focused, intuitive solitude
- Shadow Cat: Over-isolated, aloof
- Healthy Dog: Energised by bonding
- Shadow Dog: Burnt out from over-giving

Trait: Response to Stress

- Healthy Cat: Retreat, self-soothe
- Shadow Cat: Shut down, push others away
- Healthy Dog: Reach out, seek comfort

- Shadow Dog: Panic if left alone

How to Spot Them in Yourself

You may have a strong Cat archetype if you...
- Avoid phone calls or long conversations
- Feel most rested when you're alone
- Prefer depth over group interactions
- Feel overwhelmed when others "expect" emotions

You may have a strong Dog archetype if you...
- Check on others often, even at your own expense
- Struggle to let go of people or relationships
- Feel lonely even in a crowd
- Get hurt when your care isn't reciprocated

Modulation for the Cat and the Dog

Cats need to practise letting people in — without fear of losing themselves.
Dogs need to practise holding space for themselves — without guilt.

Daily Modulation Tips

For the Cat
- Share one personal emotion per day — even a small one
- Let someone help you (even if you could do it yourself)
- Invite connection instead of waiting for "safety"
- Practice soft eye contact and relaxed posture

For the Dog

- Take a break from being the caretaker
- Sit in silence and ask: "What do I need today?"
- Say no once a day — kindly and confidently
- Rest without explanation

Daily Affirmations

Cat:
- "Solitude is my strength, but I choose connection with care."
- "I am safe with people who respect my space."
- "I am open without losing myself."

Dog:
- "I give because I want to, not because I have to."
- "My worth is not tied to how much I care for others."
- "I can receive love without earning it."

When to Use Cat or Dog Energy

Use Cat energy when:
- You need focus, boundaries, or clarity
- You feel emotionally overwhelmed
- You're recovering from overstimulation

Use Dog energy when:
- You want to deepen a relationship
- You need to emotionally support or comfort someone
- You're rebuilding trust and community

VIII

The Peacock and the Rabbit – Expression vs Sensitivity

She sparkled — dressed in colour, laughter, and self-confidence.
People turned when she entered, drawn to her charm, her voice, her presence.

But across the same room, someone stood quietly by the corner — hands folded, breath measured, smile soft but hesitant.

She was a Peacock.
The other — a Rabbit.

And between them lived one of the greatest emotional struggles of our time:
"Do I show who I am — or do I stay safe?"

The Peacock – The Soul That Wants to Be Seen

The Peacock doesn't seek attention because of ego.
It seeks it because self-expression is its form of survival.

This archetype thrives when it is seen, heard, celebrated.

They speak with flair.
Dress with presence.
And shine best in environments where their creativity is encouraged.

But the shadow side?
"If I'm not seen... do I even exist?"

Core Traits of the Peacock

- Charismatic, expressive, theatrical
- Drawn to aesthetics, music, colour, and performance
- Feeds off admiration and interaction
- Struggles with insecurity when not appreciated
- Can become overly image-conscious or approval-seeking

The Rabbit – The Soul That Needs Safety

The Rabbit lives through emotional alertness.

It senses moods before they are spoken.

It reads energy with stunning accuracy.
And it withdraws — not because it doesn't care, but because it cares too much.

Rabbits are soft, wise, and deeply vulnerable.

But that vulnerability often becomes a trap of silence.
"What if being myself is what gets me hurt?"

Core Traits of the Rabbit

- Emotionally sensitive, cautious, and kind
- Feels everything — words, glances, atmospheres
- Often anxious in loud or demanding environments
- Struggles with self-trust and visibility
- Deeply loving — once safe

Healthy vs Shadow Expression

Trait: Visibility

- Healthy Peacock: Expressive, bold, magnetic
- Shadow Peacock: Approval-hungry, performative
- Healthy Rabbit: Selective, softly present
- Shadow Rabbit: Withdrawn, invisible

Trait: Emotions

- Healthy Peacock: Joyful, warm, inspiring
- Shadow Peacock: Overdramatic, reactive
- Healthy Rabbit: Empathic, intuitive
- Shadow Rabbit: Fearful, self-erasing

Trait: Self-worth

- Healthy Peacock: Self-validated, confident
- Shadow Peacock: Dependent on attention
- Healthy Rabbit: Quiet self-esteem
- Shadow Rabbit: Constant self-doubt

How to Spot These Archetypes

Peacock signs:
- You feel alive when people notice you
- You often use humour, stories, or style to connect
- You feel crushed when overlooked
- You thrive in creative, social spaces

Rabbit signs:
- You worry how others perceive you — even silently
- You notice everything, but share very little
- You're anxious in unfamiliar or chaotic environments
- You crave emotional safety above all

Modulation for the Peacock and the Rabbit

The Peacock must learn that:
"Visibility without authenticity is exhaustion."

The Rabbit must learn that:
"Silence doesn't always equal safety — expression can be healing too."

Daily Modulation Tips

For the Peacock:
- Speak truth, not performance
- Practise silence without fear of invisibility
- Create for self, not just applause
- Limit social media to strengthen internal validation

For the Rabbit:
- Say one bold sentence a day
- Practise grounding exercises in social settings
- Choose one safe person to express vulnerability
- Don't apologise for sensitivity — protect it with strength

Daily Affirmations

Peacock:
- "I shine from within — not from attention."
- "My voice matters, even when it's quiet."
- "Authenticity is my beauty."

Rabbit:
- "My sensitivity is a strength, not a weakness."
- "I am safe to speak, safe to be seen."
- "I don't need to hide to be loved."

When to Use Each Energy

Use Peacock energy when:
- You want to express, create, uplift
- You are ready to lead or present yourself
- You need to own your space unapologetically

Use Rabbit energy when:
- You need to emotionally process or heal
- You are holding space for gentleness
- You must retreat to regulate before re-engaging

IX

The Elephant and the Butterfly – Stability vs Lightness

He was the one everyone turned to in a crisis.
Calm. Unshakeable. Wise.

She was the breeze that made you smile without warning.
Colourful. Quick. Ever in motion.

One stayed to hold space.
The other fluttered through to remind everyone to breathe.

One was an Elephant.
The other — a Butterfly.

Together, they show us a vital truth:
"Healing needs both gravity and grace."

The Elephant – The Soul That Carries Generations

The Elephant carries more than its own weight.

It remembers what others forget.
It honours what others dismiss.
It stands still in storms — and often becomes the emotional rock for those around it.

But its loyalty often becomes burden.
Its wisdom becomes silence.
Its endurance becomes emotional fatigue.

"If I don't carry it, who will?" – the unspoken mantra of the Elephant.

Core Traits of the Elephant

- Deeply loyal, steady, dependable
- Carries emotional memory and ancestral wisdom
- Serves others before self
- Struggles to release pain or forgive themselves
- Feels responsible for healing the family or system

The Butterfly – The Soul That Brings Movement

The Butterfly enters with colour, possibility, and motion.

They uplift. They shift. They inspire change — but resist being tied down.

Their energy is like emotional oxygen: light, fresh, needed.

But their shadow?
"If I stop flying, will anyone still want me around?"

They often fear permanence. They flee heaviness. And they mask fear of rejection with constant reinvention.

Core Traits of the Butterfly

- Creative, spontaneous, joyful
- Quick to adapt, always exploring
- Avoids intensity and emotional heaviness
- Struggles with consistency or deep commitment
- Needs freedom to feel safe

Healthy vs Shadow Expression

Trait: Responsibility

- Healthy Elephant: Grounded, reliable, wise
- Shadow Elephant: Over-responsible, martyr
- Healthy Butterfly: Inspiring, flexible
- Shadow Butterfly: Avoidant, scattered

Trait: Emotional Depth

- Healthy Elephant: Healing presence

- Shadow Elephant: Emotionally burdened
- Healthy Butterfly: Light-hearted, mood-lifter
- Shadow Butterfly: Afraid of depth

Trait: Connection

- Healthy Elephant: Deep, long-lasting
- Shadow Elephant: Clings to outdated pain
- Healthy Butterfly: Open to new bonds
- Shadow Butterfly: Avoids commitment

How to Spot Them in You

You may be an Elephant if you...
- Feel responsible for holding the family together
- Struggle to let go of emotional wounds
- Often give advice but rarely ask for help
- Feel guilty when resting or saying no

You may be a Butterfly if you...
- Find joy in creating or expressing
- Dislike emotional heaviness or slow routines
- Move from one idea/project/person quickly
- Fear being trapped or emotionally smothered

Modulating the Elephant and the Butterfly

Elephants need to learn that:
"You can hold space without holding pain forever."

Butterflies need to learn that:
"Freedom isn't lost when you stay — it deepens."

Daily Modulation Tips

For the Elephant:
- Say no without explanation once a day
- Practise releasing guilt that isn't yours
- Ask for support without shame
- Dance, paint, or play to reawaken lightness

For the Butterfly:
- Choose one thing to complete — no matter how small
- Practise daily rituals to create grounding
- Stay with one feeling for 5 minutes without escaping
- Share your fears with someone safe

Daily Affirmations

Elephant:
- "I am not responsible for healing everyone."
- "I can be strong and still soft."
- "Letting go is also loyalty to myself."

Butterfly:
- "Freedom lives within presence, not escape."
- "My energy is valid — even when still."
- "I am loved for who I am, not just my light."

When to Use Each Energy

Use Elephant energy when:
- You are supporting others through pain
- You need deep insight or long-term stability
- You're holding emotional space with patience

Use Butterfly energy when:
- You're ready to inspire, uplift, or create
- You're navigating change or emotional heaviness
- You need to reconnect with your playful self

X

The Fox and the Whale – Clever Mask vs Deep Truth

He made everyone laugh.
Quick comebacks, effortless storytelling, always three steps ahead.

She sat quietly, listening deeply, saying little — but when she spoke, people fell silent.

He was a Fox.
She was a Whale.

Both had learned to survive...

One through distraction,
The other through depth.

The Fox – The Soul That Dodges Vulnerability

The Fox is clever — not just mentally, but emotionally.

It knows how to read a room.
It deflects discomfort with wit.
It spins stories to stay in control.

But beneath the humour, the intelligence, and the grin...
"What if they saw how scared I really am?"

The Fox hides in laughter. It camouflages its wounds in strategy.

Core Traits of the Fox

- Witty, fast-thinking, charming
- Expert at redirection and distraction
- Uses humour and stories to maintain control
- Emotionally intelligent — but struggles with honesty under pressure
- Fears exposure, rejection, or failure

The Whale – The Soul That Holds Emotional Oceans

The Whale doesn't splash.
It dives — deep, unseen, still.

This archetype holds enormous emotional wisdom.

But that depth often becomes loneliness... because few can meet them where they are.

They often say things like:
"No one really gets me."
"I'm too much — too deep, too intense, too quiet."

They don't fear vulnerability.
They fear being unheard in it.

Core Traits of the Whale

- Emotionally intense, quiet, wise
- Observes more than it speaks
- Feels others' emotions like echoes underwater
- Withdraws when unacknowledged or misunderstood
- Carries generational pain or existential awareness

Healthy vs Shadow Expression

Trait: Emotion Handling

- Healthy Fox: Adaptive, light, humorous
- Shadow Fox: Avoidant, manipulative
- Healthy Whale: Deep, healing, intuitive
- Shadow Whale: Silent, overwhelmed, shut down

Trait: Communication

- Healthy Fox: Charming, expressive
- Shadow Fox: Twists truth to escape pain
- Healthy Whale: Honest, profound, poetic
- Shadow Whale: Reclusive, emotionally numb

Trait: Coping Strategy

- Healthy Fox: Clever reframing
- Shadow Fox: Hiding pain behind humour
- Healthy Whale: Emotional grounding
- Shadow Whale: Emotional isolation

How to Spot Them in You

Fox Signs:
- You avoid emotional confrontation with humour
- You're praised for being witty or "always okay"
- You rarely show true anger or sadness
- You feel exposed when you don't have control over the narrative

Whale Signs:
- You feel everything, even what's unspoken
- You often feel misunderstood or "too deep"
- You process emotions slowly, inwardly
- You struggle to find people who meet you at your emotional depth

Modulating the Fox and the Whale

Foxes must learn:
"The truth doesn't hurt when you own it."

Whales must learn:
"Depth needs expression — or it becomes emotional drowning."

Daily Modulation Tips

For the Fox:
- Say one thing truthfully without humour each day
- Pause instead of filling every silence
- Let someone see your fear or failure
- Meditate or journal about a feeling you often avoid

For the Whale:
- Share your depth in small, consistent ways
- Ground yourself through body movement
- Reach out to someone instead of waiting to be understood
- Don't wait for perfect understanding — invite connection anyway

Daily Affirmations

Fox:
- "I am loved when I'm real — not just clever."
- "I don't need to twist to be accepted."
- "I can be honest and still be safe."

Whale:
- "My emotions are a gift — not a burden."
- "I am heard even when I feel invisible."
- "I am allowed to rise to the surface."

When to Use Each Energy

Use Fox energy when:
- You need to navigate fast-changing situations
- You are helping others break tension with humour
- You need to reframe and keep momentum

Use Whale energy when:
- You are ready to explore deep healing or truth
- You want to hold emotional space for others
- You need introspection and grounding

XI

The Bear and the Horse – Protection vs Momentum

She was the quiet strength behind her family —
Calm, watchful, rarely rushed, yet unshakably present.
When she spoke, people listened. But most of the time, she
simply was.

Her best friend, on the other hand, could never sit still.
New ventures. New places. New goals. Always in motion.

One was a Bear.
The other, a Horse.

Both had emotional strength —
But one expressed it by holding,

The other, by moving.

The Bear – The Soul That Protects by Stillness

The Bear is not lazy.
It's watchful. Wise. Intentional.

This archetype believes in protection before action.
It takes its time. It waits for the right moment.
And when it rises, it doesn't ask for permission.

But behind the Bear's strength often lies a fear:
"If I change, something might break."

So the Bear holds everything — even when it's too much.

Core Traits of the Bear

- Grounded, nurturing, quietly powerful
- Emotionally steady and stabilising
- Resists fast change or emotional chaos
- Feels responsible for protecting others
- Can become stuck, overcautious, or emotionally heavy

The Horse – The Soul That Moves to Breathe

The Horse is motion. Energy. Emotional momentum.

This archetype thrives when it's moving — physically, emotionally, or spiritually.
It seeks freedom not to run away, but to run toward life.

But when trapped or slowed?

"I feel like I'm dying inside."

The Horse needs space. It needs permission to move. Without it, it burns out or bolts.

Core Traits of the Horse

- Energetic, freedom-loving, emotionally expressive
- Thrives on change, variety, and progress
- Feels suffocated by stagnation or control
- Struggles with patience or emotional slowing down
- Can become impulsive or emotionally reactive

Healthy vs Shadow Expression

Trait: Emotional Style

- Healthy Bear: Protective, nurturing
- Shadow Bear: Controlling, stagnant
- Healthy Horse: Expressive, driven
- Shadow Horse: Impulsive, restless

Trait: Energy Flow

- Healthy Bear: Calm, deliberate
- Shadow Bear: Resistant, withdrawn
- Healthy Horse: Motivated, bold
- Shadow Horse: Unpredictable, burnout-prone

Trait: Relationship Role

- Healthy Bear: Guardian, steady presence
- Shadow Bear: Overbearing, passive-aggressive

- Healthy Horse: Inspiring, energising
- Shadow Horse: Avoidant, non-committal

How to Spot These Archetypes

Bear Signs:
- You often feel the need to "hold the fort"
- You take time to trust, but once you do, you stay
- You dislike chaos or sudden changes
- You rarely express emotions quickly — you carry them silently

Horse Signs:
- You feel most alive when you're exploring something new
- You're easily bored by repetition or overthinking
- You process emotions through movement or action
- You resist control — especially emotional control

Modulating the Bear and the Horse

Bears must learn:
"Stillness can nurture — but not if it stops growth."

Horses must learn:
"Movement is healing — but only when it's conscious, not reactionary."

Daily Modulation Tips

For the Bear:
- Say yes to something spontaneous
- Let go of one role or burden you've outgrown

- Move your body in a new way — break the physical stillness
- Ask: "What do I need to release today?"

For the Horse:
- Practise stillness through breathwork or quiet reflection
- Stick with one feeling — don't outrun it
- Slow down your reaction by 5 seconds
- Ask: "Am I running toward something, or away from discomfort?"

Daily Affirmations

Bear:
- "I protect — but I don't have to carry it all."
- "Stillness is sacred, but I am safe to change."
- "My presence is power."

Horse:
- "My movement is meaningful."
- "I am safe to stay present, even in stillness."
- "Freedom lives in emotional balance."

When to Use Each Energy

Use Bear energy when:
- You need to hold emotional space
- You're supporting others through fear or change
- You are grounding into stability and inner strength

Use Horse energy when:
- You need to push through stagnation or stuckness
- You are ready to act with heart and clarity
- You want to reignite purpose and passion

XII

The Eagle and the Camel – Vision vs Endurance

He always seemed above it all —
Focused. Detached. Never caught in the noise.
People looked to him for strategy, not sympathy.

She, on the other hand, never complained.
She kept going.
Even when life gave her nothing to work with, she kept
showing up — quietly, faithfully.

He was an Eagle.
She was a Camel.

One saw beyond.

The other survived within.

The Eagle – The Soul That Sees Beyond

The Eagle is a visionary.
It detaches not out of coldness, but for clarity.

Eagles rise above the storm.
They don't get caught in emotional quicksand.
They observe, zoom out, and move only when purpose calls.

But beneath this powerful detachment often lies a shadow:
"If I feel too much, I might lose focus."

So they learn to numb emotion... and call it strength.

Core Traits of the Eagle

- Clear, focused, visionary
- Emotionally minimal, mentally sharp
- High standards for self and others
- Leads best with distance and independence
- May come off as cold, unreachable, or perfectionistic

The Camel – The Soul That Survives the Desert

The Camel walks — silently and faithfully.

This archetype is the survivor that never asks for applause.
It endures emotional droughts. It stores what it needs.
It keeps going when others collapse.

But its pain is often this:

"Why do I only get noticed when I break?"

Camels don't expect luxury. They expect nothing.
And sometimes, that's the problem.

Core Traits of the Camel

- Emotionally self-sufficient
- High endurance, low emotional demand
- Rarely expresses needs — may not even recognise them
- Carries burdens without asking for help
- Struggles with joy, permission to receive, or emotional richness

Healthy vs Shadow Expression

Trait: Vision

- Healthy Eagle: Clear, high-focus
- Shadow Eagle: Detached, arrogant
- Healthy Camel: Steady, strong
- Shadow Camel: Emotionally suppressed

Trait: Coping Style

- Healthy Eagle: Observation, zoom-out
- Shadow Eagle: Avoidance, isolation
- Healthy Camel: Quiet resilience
- Shadow Camel: Resignation, numbness

Trait: Needs Expression

- Healthy Eagle: Rare but clear

- Shadow Eagle: Non-existent
- Healthy Camel: Delayed or denied
- Shadow Camel: Hidden to the point of harm

How to Spot These Archetypes

Eagle Signs:
- You see through emotions and straight into patterns
- You dislike drama or excessive emotional sharing
- You withdraw when overwhelmed — to "analyse, not feel"
- People admire your clarity but often feel intimidated

Camel Signs:
- You rarely ask for help
- You feel deeply but don't know how to show it
- You are seen as "strong" by everyone — even when you're struggling
- You have a high pain tolerance — emotionally and physically

Modulating the Eagle and the Camel

Eagles must learn:
"Emotion doesn't blur your vision — it deepens it."

Camels must learn:
"Endurance is noble, but receiving is healing."

Daily Modulation Tips

For the Eagle:
- Share one emotion daily without analysing it

- Pause your strategic thinking — and just feel
- Practise closeness with someone you trust
- Notice when independence is actually fear of vulnerability

For the Camel:
- Say what you need — even if it feels strange
- Allow someone to help you with a simple task
- Reflect: "Where am I enduring what I no longer need to?"
- Practise small pleasures — and allow yourself to feel joy

Daily Affirmations

Eagle:
- "My emotions are not a weakness — they are clarity in another form."
- "I can feel and still lead."
- "My strength is not just in my mind, but in my heart."

Camel:
- "I deserve rest, joy, and nourishment — not just survival."
- "My endurance is sacred, but so is my right to be cared for."
- "I am not invisible just because I am quiet."

When to Use Each Energy

Use Eagle energy when:
- You need focus, clarity, or higher decision-making
- You must detach to plan or lead without bias
- You're navigating crisis with calm

Use Camel energy when:
- You are enduring long-term emotional or physical strain
- You must hold space with humility and patience
- You're rebuilding slowly after loss

XIII

The Tiger and the Spider – Power vs Precision

He stormed into the discussion.
Sharp, bold, unstoppable. His words were fire — full of conviction, no filters.

She, however, sat back. Quiet.
Watching everything. Saying little.
But when she moved, it shifted the entire direction of the conversation.

He was a Tiger.
She was a Spider.

Both powerful.

But one used force.
The other, finesse.

The Tiger – The Soul That Charges

Tigers are emotional warriors.
They don't wait. They act.
They fight for what they believe in — immediately, loudly, fearlessly.

They value honour, loyalty, and momentum.

But when emotionally imbalanced?
"If I don't roar, I won't be respected."

That belief drives them to overexert, overreact, or overpower.

Core Traits of the Tiger

- Bold, courageous, protective
- High emotional intensity
- Responds fast — physically or verbally
- Intolerant of delays, betrayal, or injustice
- Can become dominating, impulsive, or destructive

The Spider – The Soul That Weaves in Silence

The Spider doesn't chase.
It waits. It watches. It calculates.

It's not cold — it's consciously in control.

Spiders are often misunderstood as manipulative.
But in truth, they simply see what others miss.

Their fear is:
"If I reveal too soon, I'll lose all control."

So they withhold, micromanage, or spin emotional webs to feel safe.

Core Traits of the Spider

- Highly perceptive, emotionally restrained
- Controls outcomes through planning, not power
- Avoids direct confrontation — prefers indirect influence
- Can become suspicious, withdrawn, or overly calculated
- Thrives in quiet leadership or systems thinking

Healthy vs Shadow Expression

Trait: Response Style

- Healthy Tiger: Brave, decisive, assertive
- Shadow Tiger: Aggressive, forceful
- Healthy Spider: Strategic, composed
- Shadow Spider: Manipulative, controlling

Trait: Emotional Control

- Healthy Tiger: Channelled intensity
- Shadow Tiger: Reactive outbursts
- Healthy Spider: Observant, patient
- Shadow Spider: Emotionally closed off

Trait: Relational Style

- Healthy Tiger: Protective, loyal
- Shadow Tiger: Possessive, intimidating
- Healthy Spider: Subtle, guiding
- Shadow Spider: Secretive, distant

How to Spot These Archetypes

Tiger Signs:
- You act first, reflect later
- You protect loved ones fiercely — sometimes too much
- You hate feeling powerless
- You often regret things said in anger or intensity

Spider Signs:
- You rarely show your full thoughts or feelings
- You like being in control — especially emotionally
- You observe others deeply but don't reveal yourself
- You feel safest when pulling strings behind the scenes

Modulating the Tiger and the Spider

Tigers must learn:
"Power isn't how loud you are — it's how wisely you use your strength."

Spiders must learn:
"Trust is not control — it's the courage to be transparent."

Daily Modulation Tips

For the Tiger:
- Pause 10 seconds before reacting
- Practise breathwork during emotional surges
- Direct your intensity into physical activity (exercise, dance, martial arts)
- Ask: "Is this battle worth my energy?"

For the Spider:
- Say something you were planning to withhold
- Ask directly instead of hinting
- Let someone else lead or decide
- Journal about a truth you haven't voiced

Daily Affirmations

Tiger:
- "My strength is grounded in wisdom."
- "I don't need to roar to be heard."
- "I choose power, not pressure."

Spider:
- "I don't need control to feel safe."
- "My truth deserves space, not secrecy."
- "I connect clearly — not just cleverly."

When to Use Each Energy

Use Tiger energy when:
- You need to defend, act fast, or break inertia
- You're standing up for someone or something important
- You must push through resistance or fear

Use Spider energy when:
- You're managing systems or leading behind the scenes
- You're navigating emotionally complex situations
- You're planning, designing, or analysing long-term change

XIV

The Hawk and the Raven – Focus vs Depth

He was the kind of person who made you feel like a goal.
Laser-focused, intensely driven, always aiming for something bigger.
Nothing escaped his attention — except, maybe, his own emotions.

She was the mystery.
She'd say just one sentence — and it would echo for hours.
Not loud, not linear — but deeply felt.

He was a Hawk.
She was a Raven.

Both saw things no one else could.
But one sought targets.
The other, truth.

The Hawk – The Soul That Seeks Focus

The Hawk is the high-flyer.
It sees clearly.
It picks a target.
And it doesn't stop until it gets there.

This archetype is about goals, purpose, and clarity.
But in its shadow, it becomes rigid — chasing achievement while ignoring emotional depth.

"If I lose focus, I lose myself."
So the Hawk flies forward — but forgets to look inward.

Core Traits of the Hawk

- Intensely goal-oriented and driven
- High clarity, ambition, and personal standards
- Motivated by vision and long-term success
- May struggle with flexibility or emotional complexity
- Can become impatient, judgmental, or emotionally cold

The Raven – The Soul That Sees Symbolism

The Raven doesn't hunt — it wanders.
It sees between the lines. It speaks in symbols. It holds the mysteries others avoid.

The Raven isn't focused on results — it's focused on

meaning.

"What you see is not all that there is."

They live in nuance. And they fear being misunderstood more than they fear failure.

Core Traits of the Raven

- Deep, mystical, emotionally intelligent
- Comfortable in the unknown, shadow, or paradox
- Introspective and often poetic
- Struggles with structure, timelines, or goal-based systems
- Can appear vague, lost in thought, or emotionally intense

Healthy vs Shadow Expression

Trait: Thinking Style

- Healthy Hawk: Sharp, decisive, clear
- Shadow Hawk: Rigid, black-and-white
- Healthy Raven: Symbolic, insightful
- Shadow Raven: Confused, overly abstract

Trait: Emotional Style

- Healthy Hawk: Cool, focused, disciplined
- Shadow Hawk: Detached, suppressive
- Healthy Raven: Reflective, layered
- Shadow Raven: Melancholic, brooding

Trait: Purpose Style

- Healthy Hawk: Goal-oriented, visionary
- Shadow Hawk: Obsessed, results-only
- Healthy Raven: Purpose-driven by intuition
- Shadow Raven: Unstructured, lost

How to Spot These Archetypes

Hawk Signs:
- You define success clearly and pursue it without distractions
- You feel uneasy without a target or next milestone
- You dislike emotional complexity — prefer logic and clarity
- You're often told you're "too intense" or "too much in your head"

Raven Signs:
- You sense things that others miss — emotionally or spiritually
- You value meaning over speed or outcomes
- You feel deeply but may not express clearly
- You're often seen as "deep," "weird," or "hard to read"

Modulating the Hawk and the Raven

Hawks must learn:
"Vision without flexibility leads to burnout."

Ravens must learn:
"Depth without clarity leads to confusion."

Daily Modulation Tips

For the Hawk:
- Take one day without a to-do list
- Meditate without a goal — let yourself just be
- Ask someone: "What do you feel about this?" before deciding
- Reflect: "What am I avoiding by chasing?"

For the Raven:
- Write one structured thought or plan each day
- Share your insights — don't just feel them
- Break big emotions into language
- Commit to one simple action, even if it's imperfect

Daily Affirmations

Hawk:
- "My clarity includes my heart."
- "Resting is not failure."
- "Focus is powerful — but flexibility is wise."

Raven:
- "My depth is my gift — and I am allowed to express it."
- "I can bring light to the shadows I understand."
- "Being misunderstood is not the end — it's an invitation to speak."

When to Use Each Energy

Use Hawk energy when:
- You're building structure or chasing a clear goal
- You need direction and clarity
- You're navigating chaos and need a plan

Use Raven energy when:
- You're sitting with emotional or spiritual depth
- You need creative or intuitive insight
- You're helping others move through trauma or the unknown

XV

The Frog and the Wolf – Transition vs Loyalty

She cried during change — even when it was good.
New city, new job, even new clothes — everything felt like a loss.
But she always came out of it wiser, softer, freer.

He wasn't like that.
He stayed. He protected. He remembered birthdays.
You could trust him with your past — because he never forgot it.

She was a Frog.
He was a Wolf.

She taught us how to move on.
He reminded us where we came from.

The Frog – The Soul That Transforms

The Frog is about emotional evolution.

It changes not once — but many times.
It feels everything.
And it needs time to process those feelings through phases.

Frogs often live between who they were and who they are becoming.

"I'm scared to change — but I'm more scared to stay stuck."

They cry. They leap. They adapt.
But they need emotional space to do so.

Core Traits of the Frog

- Emotionally sensitive and responsive
- Goes through intense emotional and identity transitions
- Feels grief even in positive changes
- Struggles with decisions and endings
- Often rebirths into new phases of self with each cycle

The Wolf – The Soul That Remembers

The Wolf is not loud.
But you'll know it by its loyalty.

This archetype stays — even when things get hard.

It remembers. It guards. It honours emotional territory.

Wolves are about community, memory, and emotional rootedness.

"Leaving isn't always brave. Staying is, too."

They are fierce in love — but may fear betrayal so deeply that they shut out change altogether.

Core Traits of the Wolf

- Fiercely loyal, emotionally protective
- Trusts slowly, but defends deeply
- Values tradition, bonds, and honour
- Struggles with letting go or moving forward
- Can become emotionally territorial or guarded

Healthy vs Shadow Expression

Trait: Change Style

- Healthy Frog: Adaptive, intuitive
- Shadow Frog: Overwhelmed, indecisive
- Healthy Wolf: Grounded, committed
- Shadow Wolf: Stuck, controlling

Trait: Emotional Style

- Healthy Frog: Soft, expressive
- Shadow Frog: Draining, inconsistent
- Healthy Wolf: Loyal, protective
- Shadow Wolf: Possessive, emotionally rigid

Trait: Relationship Role

- Healthy Frog: Evolves with honesty
- Shadow Frog: Flees discomfort
- Healthy Wolf: Bonds for life
- Shadow Wolf: Shuts out new connections

How to Spot These Archetypes

Frog Signs:
- You cry often during transition — even happy ones
- You constantly feel like you're between versions of yourself
- You feel "too much" in moments others rush through
- You fear change but feel compelled by it

Wolf Signs:
- You never forget a kindness or betrayal
- You stay longer than most in relationships or commitments
- You feel emotionally responsible for those you love
- You struggle to open up to new people or ideas

Modulating the Frog and the Wolf

Frogs must learn:
"Every transformation needs emotional grounding."

Wolves must learn:
"Loyalty is strength — but flexibility is survival."

Daily Modulation Tips

For the Frog:
- Name the emotion you're feeling mid-transition
- Practise holding both joy and grief without guilt
- Celebrate small progress — not just outcomes
- Journal: "What part of me is dying? What part is being born?"

For the Wolf:
- Reflect: "Am I staying because of love or fear?"
- Try something unfamiliar with someone you trust
- Share a memory with someone new
- Loosen one rigid emotional rule you've followed too long

Daily Affirmations

Frog:
- "I honour my feelings — even when they change."
- "I evolve gently, with purpose."
- "I am safe in transition."

Wolf:
- "My loyalty is my strength — not my cage."
- "I can love the past and still embrace the future."
- "I trust myself to let go when needed."

When to Use Each Energy

Use Frog energy when:
- You're moving through emotional, spiritual, or identity shifts
- You're healing, growing, or making major life decisions

- You need permission to feel all your phases

Use Wolf energy when:
- You're protecting what matters most
- You're building trust, connection, and commitment
- You need to anchor into emotional loyalty

XVI

The Phoenix – The Fire That Burns to Rebuild

They said she was "too intense."

That she changed too much.
That her life was one transformation after another.

They didn't see the ashes she rose from.
They didn't feel the fire she had to walk through.

She wasn't unstable.
She was a Phoenix.

The Phoenix – The Soul That Must Die to Be Reborn

The Phoenix archetype lives through emotional combustion.
It doesn't just "change" — it destroys what no longer serves.

This soul sets fire to comfort.
Not out of recklessness — but because it knows that true life requires constant resurrection.

"I am not the same person I was yesterday — and I'm proud of that."

Core Traits of the Phoenix

- Intense, spiritual, radically transformative
- Experiences life through cycles of death and rebirth
- Often misunderstood for instability or emotional drama
- Sheds relationships, identities, careers — anything that limits growth
- Deeply powerful, but prone to loneliness or periods of inner chaos

Healthy vs Shadow Expression

Trait: Change Style

- Healthy Phoenix: Transformational, wise
- Shadow Phoenix: Destructive, dramatic

Trait: Emotional Flow

- Healthy Phoenix: Cathartic, powerful
- Shadow Phoenix: Volatile, overwhelming

Trait: Relational Style

- Healthy Phoenix: Honest, soul-deep connections
- Shadow Phoenix: Chaotic, always ending cycles

How to Spot the Phoenix in You

- You often feel that your "old self" no longer fits
- You have been through many versions of yourself — sometimes after emotional collapse
- You feel emotions intensely and fully — even when they break you
- You've rebuilt yourself multiple times — stronger, wiser, deeper

Modulating the Phoenix

Phoenixes must learn:
"You don't need to burn everything to begin again."

Their gift is transformation.
But their challenge is learning to transition without total destruction.

Daily Modulation Tips

- Ask: "Can I transform this gently instead of burning it down?"
- Practise grounding during emotional surges (breath,

nature, ritual)
- Honour your endings with gratitude, not guilt
- Reflect: "What am I being invited to rise into — not just out from?"

Daily Affirmations

- "My power lies in rebirth, not reaction."
- "I rise with purpose — not pain."
- "I can honour endings without self-destruction."
- "My story is sacred. Every version of me mattered."
- "I am not broken. I am becoming."

When to Use Phoenix Energy

- You're facing a major life transition, loss, or identity shift
- You feel stuck in something that no longer reflects who you are
- You're ready to release, heal, and fully become
- You want to guide others through deep transformation

PART III

The Modulation Method

"This is the toolkit. Here you teach readers how to shift archetypal energy through awareness, bridging, journaling, daily rituals, compatibility mapping, cognitive reframing, and the Golden Mean."

XVII
What Is Modulation?

*If discovering your archetype is the
first awakening,
modulation is the act of mastering it.*

Archetype Modulation Therapy (AMT) is not about labelling who you are.
It's about guiding who you're becoming — by refining the traits that serve you and transforming those that sabotage you.

We are all born with dominant archetypes.
But our power lies not in being stuck with one,
It lies in learning how to balance it, and when needed, blend it.

This is modulation.

The Two-Step Modulation Process

Modulation is not random transformation.
It follows a precise inner method:

STEP 1: Balance the Archetype Using the Golden Mean

Every archetype has a:
- Bright side (its healthiest expression)
- Shadow side (its distortion in excess or deficiency)

Using the concept of Aristotle's Golden Mean, we learn:
"Every virtue lies between two extremes."

For example:

Archetype – Deficiency / Golden Mean / Excess
   Lion

- Deficiency: Passivity
- Golden Mean (Bright): Assertive Leadership
- Excess: Dominance

   Owl

- Deficiency: Confused dreaming
- Golden Mean (Bright): Insightful Observation
- Excess: Paranoia / Overthinking

Rabbit

- Deficiency: Numb avoidance
- Golden Mean (Bright): Healthy Sensitivity
- Excess: Anxiety / Hyperalertness

The first act of modulation is not to "become something else."

It is to return to the centre of your own archetype — where its power flows without pain.

☙

STEP 2: Add a Compatible Archetype as Support

After returning to balance, life may still demand more.
More courage. More flexibility. More strategy. More softness.

That's where modulation add-ons come in.

You consciously integrate traits of a compatible archetype to support your emotional challenge.

Modulation is not abandonment. It's enhancement.

Example:
- A Rabbit in fear of social judgement may add traits of the Dolphin for joy and social fluidity.
- A Snake stuck in survival might benefit from blending with the Owl for insight and detachment.

When Direct Modulation Fails: The Bridge Archetype

Not all archetypes play well together.

You may find that your core and desired archetype are incompatible — either in traits, values, or emotional wiring.

This doesn't mean transformation is impossible.
It means you need a bridge.

A bridge archetype is one that shares traits with both ends of the transformation, helping you transition safely.

Example:
- A Rabbit cannot shift directly into Lion energy.
- But it may first blend with Dog (support + protection), which bridges Rabbit's sensitivity with Lion's strength.

Full Definition of Modulation (AMT)

Archetype Modulation =
1. Transforming shadow to bright using the Golden Mean
2. Blending a compatible archetype, either directly or through a bridge archetype

Why Modulation Is the Core of Healing

You are not fixed.
You are not broken.
You are modulatable.

Whether you are a healer, a leader, a creator, or a survivor
—

your archetype is your emotional engine.

AMT teaches you how to:
- Identify your pattern
- Balance your energy
- Blend what's needed
- Bridge what feels impossible

This is how archetypes stop defining you... and start refining you.

XVIII

Modulation Toolkit – Reframing the Beliefs of Every Archetype

Lion

- Shadow Belief: If I don't dominate, I'll be disrespected.
- Bright Belief: True leadership inspires, not intimidates.
- Modulation Cue: My power grows when I listen and lead with calm.

Elephant

- Shadow Belief: I must carry everyone's pain.
- Bright Belief: I can support others without losing myself.
- Modulation Cue: I release what's not mine to hold.

Owl

- Shadow Belief: Overthinking protects me from failure.
- Bright Belief: Clarity comes from both thought and action.
- Modulation Cue: Insight serves best when paired with flow.

Fox

- Shadow Belief: I must hide my truth to stay safe.
- Bright Belief: Honesty connects me more than strategy ever will.
- Modulation Cue: My truth is more powerful than my performance.

Snake

- Shadow Belief: If I trust, I'll be destroyed.

- Bright Belief: Caution is strength — but trust is power.
- Modulation Cue: Not everyone is a threat. I choose wisely.

Dolphin

- Shadow Belief: If I stop smiling, they won't love me.
- Bright Belief: My joy is real when it includes my truth.
- Modulation Cue: I am lovable even in silence and sadness.

Cat

- Shadow Belief: Needing others makes me weak.
- Bright Belief: Solitude is strength — but connection is nourishment.
- Modulation Cue: I can ask, receive, and still be free.

Dog

- Shadow Belief: If I don't serve, I'll be abandoned.
- Bright Belief: I am worthy of love beyond usefulness.
- Modulation Cue: Loyalty begins with me being loyal to myself.

Peacock

- Shadow Belief: If I'm not dazzling, I'll be invisible.
- Bright Belief: My presence matters — even without performance.
- Modulation Cue: I shine from authenticity, not applause.

Whale

- Shadow Belief: I'm too much — so I'll stay silent.
- Bright Belief: My depth is healing when expressed with trust.
- Modulation Cue: I am safe to be fully seen.

Phoenix

- Shadow Belief: Destruction is the only way to change.
- Bright Belief: Transformation can be tender and deliberate.
- Modulation Cue: I can rise without burning everything down.

Frog

- Shadow Belief: I will lose myself in change.

- Bright Belief: I grow through change — not away from myself.
- Modulation Cue: I evolve without erasing who I was.

Rabbit

- Shadow Belief: The world is dangerous — I must stay alert or be hurt.
- Bright Belief: Sensitivity is strength when grounded in self-trust.
- Modulation Cue: I am safe to feel and flourish.

Tiger

- Shadow Belief: I must fight to earn respect.
- Bright Belief: Power speaks clearest through purpose, not pressure.
- Modulation Cue: I lead with clarity, not chaos.

Horse

- Shadow Belief: Commitment is a trap.
- Bright Belief: Freedom deepens when paired with purpose.
- Modulation Cue: I am free — and still focused.

Butterfly

- Shadow Belief: If I stay, I'll be trapped.
- Bright Belief: Creativity thrives in presence, not escape.
- Modulation Cue: My lightness is strongest when rooted.

Spider

- Shadow Belief: Control is the only way to feel safe.
- Bright Belief: True power comes from transparency.
- Modulation Cue: I weave influence with honesty, not fear.

Eagle

- Shadow Belief: Emotions blur my clarity.
- Bright Belief: My vision sharpens when it includes my heart.
- Modulation Cue: Feeling does not dilute — it deepens my focus.

Camel

- Shadow Belief: Needing rest is weakness.

- Bright Belief: Sustainability comes from rhythm, not denial.
- Modulation Cue: I am worthy of ease — not just survival.

Raven

- Shadow Belief: If they don't understand me, I must stay hidden.
- Bright Belief: Mystery is medicine when I share it with care.
- Modulation Cue: I give voice to the shadow with wisdom.

Wolf

- Shadow Belief: If I let go, I'll lose everything.
- Bright Belief: Loyalty is sacred when it evolves with love.
- Modulation Cue: I honour the past — and trust the future.

Hawk

- Shadow Belief: If I lose control, I lose everything.
- Bright Belief: Precision is powerful when held with softness.
- Modulation Cue: I aim with focus — and adjust with grace.

Bear

- Shadow Belief: If I don't carry it, no one will.
- Bright Belief: Strength means knowing when to rest.
- Modulation Cue: I protect — but I also pause.

Cognitive Distortions in Archetype Shadows

Lion

Common Cognitive Distortions:

- Should Statements
- Labelling
- All-or-Nothing Thinking

Elephant

Common Cognitive Distortions:

- Emotional Reasoning
- Overgeneralisation

Owl

Common Cognitive Distortions:

- Mental Filtering
- Overgeneralisation

Fox

Common Cognitive Distortions:

- Mind Reading
- Fortune Telling

Snake

Common Cognitive Distortions:

- Catastrophising
- Magnification

Dolphin

Common Cognitive Distortions:

- Minimisation
- Emotional Reasoning

Cat

Common Cognitive Distortions:

- All-or-Nothing Thinking
- Personalisation

Dog

Common Cognitive Distortions:

- People Pleasing (Personalisation)

- Labelling

Peacock

Common Cognitive Distortions:

- Approval Addiction
- Should Statements

Whale

Common Cognitive Distortions:

- Emotional Reasoning
- Filtering

Phoenix

Common Cognitive Distortions:

- Catastrophising
- Black-and-White Thinking

Frog

Common Cognitive Distortions:

- Overgeneralisation
- Emotional Reasoning

Rabbit

Common Cognitive Distortions:

- Catastrophising
- Mind Reading

Tiger

Common Cognitive Distortions:

- Should Statements
- Labelling

Horse

Common Cognitive Distortions:

- All-or-Nothing Thinking
- Avoidance

Butterfly

Common Cognitive Distortions:

- Disqualifying the Positive
- Escapism

Spider

Common Cognitive Distortions:

- Control Fallacy
- Mind Reading

Eagle

Common Cognitive Distortions:

- Minimisation of Emotion
- Labelling

Camel

Common Cognitive Distortions:

- Should Statements
- Filtering

Raven

Common Cognitive Distortions:

- Emotional Reasoning
- Magical Thinking

Wolf

Common Cognitive Distortions:

- Overgeneralisation
- All-or-Nothing Thinking

Hawk

Common Cognitive Distortions:

- Perfectionism
- Filtering

Bear

Common Cognitive Distortions:

- Personalisation
- Control Fallacy

XIX

Your Blended Persona – How Archetypes Combine, Conflict, and Collaborate

We are not made of a single song.

We are symphonies — layered, complex, beautiful — sometimes harmonious, sometimes chaotic.

And if this book has shown you anything, let it be this:

You are not one archetype. You are a blend.
A combination of stories, instincts, moods, and memories.
You are the fire of the Phoenix and the stillness of the

Whale.
The charm of the Peacock and the clarity of the Eagle.

This is what Archetype Modulation Therapy (AMT) gives you. Not just awareness of your inner animal... but the art of blending them.

Because the real magic happens when these forces learn to dance.

COMPATIBLE ARCHETYPES:
When Energy Amplifies
Some archetypes are meant to walk together.
They hold each other like hands in a prayer — different, but unified.

· Lion + Owl → Leadership with wisdom
· Dolphin + Rabbit → Joyful healing with gentle sensitivity
· Phoenix + Whale → Transformation with depth and grace
· Elephant + Bear → Stability with grounded protection
· Fox + Cat → Playful wit with intuitive silence

Your personality doesn't just make sense — it feels like home.

INCOMPATIBLE ARCHETYPES:
When Energy Collides
· Tiger + Rabbit → Courage vs Fear
· Peacock + Camel → Showmanship vs Simplicity
· Spider + Dolphin → Strategy vs Vulnerability
· Cat + Dog → Detachment vs Devotion
· Phoenix + Bear → Change vs Preservation

These archetypes don't make you wrong. They make you human. But blending them directly is like mixing fire and ice — they need something more...

BRIDGE ARCHETYPES:

aking the Impossible Possible

Bridge archetypes are emotional adapters — they carry pieces of both energies and allow them to meet halfway.

- Phoenix and Cat → Use Whale (depth with containment)
- Tiger and Rabbit → Use Dog (courage with gentleness)
- Spider and Dolphin → Use Fox (tactical playfulness)
- Peacock and Camel → Use Butterfly (simple creativity)
- Eagle and Rabbit → Use Owl (vision tempered with care)

YOUR BLENDED PERSONA IN ACTION

Ask yourself:

1. What is my dominant archetype right now?
2. What energy am I craving or resisting?
3. Do they naturally support or conflict?
4. Is there a bridge I can introduce to ease this blend?
5. What ritual can I do today to ground this modulation?

Let each action you take become a love letter to your blended self.

YOU ARE A LIVING SYSTEM

This chapter is your permission slip:

- To contain opposites.
- To shift identities without losing truth.
- To blend complexity without falling apart.

You are not a *fixed type*. You are a conscious blend of emotional intelligences.
You are not one. You are many in harmony.

This is your ***Blended Persona*** — the result of insight, acceptance, and modulation.
And when your archetypes begin to collaborate rather than collide, you don't just live better.

You become **WHOLE**.

Bridge Archetype Map – Practitioner's Guide to Modulation Transitions

Not all archetypes can shift directly into another. Sometimes, emotional structure, core beliefs, or energy frequency are simply too divergent.

That's where the Bridge Archetype comes in — a transitional emotional form that:
- Shares partial traits with both archetypes
- Creates emotional safety during change
- Allows gradual integration of traits that would otherwise overwhelm or conflict

Use this map to support clients who are stuck between who they are... and who they are becoming.

Lion

Incompatible With: Whale, Raven, Rabbit
    Recommended Bridges: Dog, Owl, Tiger

Elephant

Incompatible With: Tiger, Spider
    Recommended Bridges: Bear, Owl

Owl

Incompatible With: Butterfly, Tiger
    Recommended Bridges: Eagle, Spider

Fox

Incompatible With: Dog, Phoenix
Recommended Bridges: Cat, Snake

Snake

Incompatible With: Dolphin, Dog, Rabbit
Recommended Bridges: Owl, Fox

Dolphin

Incompatible With: Snake, Spider
Recommended Bridges: Rabbit, Butterfly

Cat

Incompatible With: Dog, Peacock
Recommended Bridges: Owl, Fox

Dog

Incompatible With: Snake, Cat
Recommended Bridges: Rabbit, Bear

Peacock

Incompatible With: Eagle, Camel, Cat
Recommended Bridges: Butterfly, Dolphin

Whale

Incompatible With: Lion, Spider

Recommended Bridges: Elephant, Frog

Phoenix

Incompatible With: Bear, Horse, Cat
Recommended Bridges: Frog, Raven

Frog

Incompatible With: Tiger, Eagle
Recommended Bridges: Whale, Phoenix

Rabbit

Incompatible With: Tiger, Spider, Hawk
Recommended Bridges: Dog, Dolphin

Tiger

Incompatible With: Rabbit, Cat, Whale
Recommended Bridges: Horse, Lion

Horse

Incompatible With: Phoenix, Bear
Recommended Bridges: Hawk, Butterfly

Butterfly

Incompatible With: Owl, Camel
Recommended Bridges: Dolphin, Horse

Spider

Incompatible With: Dolphin, Rabbit
Recommended Bridges: Fox, Owl

Eagle

Incompatible With: Peacock, Frog
Recommended Bridges: Owl, Hawk

Camel

Incompatible With: Peacock, Butterfly
Recommended Bridges: Bear, Elephant

Raven

Incompatible With: Lion, Tiger
Recommended Bridges: Whale, Phoenix

Wolf

Incompatible With: Owl, Cat
Recommended Bridges: Dog, Bear

Hawk

Incompatible With: Rabbit, Whale
Recommended Bridges: Eagle, Horse

Bear

Incompatible With: Phoenix, Peacock
Recommended Bridges: Elephant, Camel

XX
You Are More Than One Animal

You were never meant to fit in a single skin.

Not a Lion every day.
Not a Dolphin in every moment.
Not even the Phoenix — all the time.

You are not one animal.
You are a living ecosystem of archetypes.

And learning how to honour all of them — even the ones
that seem contradictory — is the real mastery.

You Are a System, Not a Symptom

Traditional personality typing often tells you what box you're in.
But life is not a box — it's a forest.

Some days, your inner Tiger rises in strength.
Other days, your inner Rabbit shivers in fear.
Both are you.

The more you accept, the more you modulate.
You do not become someone else. You become more of who you already are.

You Will Change, and That's Not a Flaw

If you feel different in different environments — good.
If you used to be one way and now feel another — excellent.

AMT does not demand consistency.
It invites coherence.

"I am still me — even when I shift shapes."

The Inner Conflicts Will Soften

Many of us were taught that contradictions are bad.

That you can't be:

- Both strong and sensitive
- Both loyal and independent
- Both structured and spontaneous

But in AMT, integration is the goal.

Each archetype you honour becomes part of your wisdom — not your confusion.

You Are Your Own Formula

This is the ultimate truth of AMT:

You are not one animal.
You are a constellation.

You are:
- The Lion who leads
- The Snake who survives
- The Butterfly who creates
- The Phoenix who rises
- The Whale who feels
- The Owl who sees

...and more.

There is no limit to who you can become,
as long as you are becoming with awareness.

Final Reflection Questions

- What archetypes have shaped your past?
- Which ones helped you survive?
- Which ones are asking to come forward now?
- What part of you have you exiled — and how can you invite it back?

The Future of Modulation

This book was a beginning.
But your journey into archetype work continues.

Modulate. Reflect. Grow.
And above all — never shrink to fit a single role again.

XXI

What Happens When You Master Modulate

Modulation is not just a concept. It's a catalyst.

Once you learn how to shift your archetypes with awareness, your life doesn't just improve — it transforms.

This chapter brings real-world reflections from those who applied AMT — in health, relationships, career, and self-worth.

Each story reflects what happens when you stop asking, "What's wrong with me?"

And start asking, "Which part of me needs modulation?"

૪૦

1. *From Rabbit to Dolphin: Healing Social Anxiety*

Nisha was a quiet 24-year-old postgraduate student who dreaded group projects.
She felt constantly watched, judged, and inadequate. Her inner world was full of brilliant ideas — but no one saw them.

Her dominant archetype was Rabbit, stuck in shadow hyperalertness.

Modulation Steps:
- Step 1: Ground her Rabbit with affirmations of safety.
- Step 2: Add the Dolphin for lightness and ease in expression.

Within 3 months:
- She initiated two presentations.
- She stopped apologising for speaking.
- She laughed — in public — without shame.

"I didn't need to change myself. I just needed to remember how to play."

2. *From Snake to Owl: Repairing Relationship Control*

Anand, a 40-year-old entrepreneur, came to AMT with the words:

"I sabotage every relationship that gets close."

His Snake archetype was in survival mode — always doubting, always controlling.

Modulation Steps:
- From Snake's shadow: "If I don't control, I'll be betrayed"
- To Owl's insight: "I can observe without assuming harm"

He learned to:
- Pause before interrogating his partner
- Name his fears aloud
- Create trust through transparency, not testing

"I thought my fear protected me. Now I know wisdom protects better."

ॐ

3. From Butterfly to Horse: Finding Direction

Priya was a creative spirit who jumped from project to project.
Poetry. Podcasts. Pottery. Nothing lasted more than a month.

She identified as a Butterfly, but her shadow was in full effect: avoidance of roots.

Modulation:
- Honour creativity without escaping responsibility.
- Add the Horse archetype for direction and commitment.

Results:
- Launched a wellness startup
- Completed projects consistently
- Still feels free — but now with purpose

"I didn't clip my wings. I gave them a destination."

4. From Phoenix to Camel: Emotional Stability After Burnout

A 32-year-old therapist said:
"I feel like I keep burning my life down and calling it growth."

Her dominant archetype was Phoenix — rich in trauma healing, but prone to emotional collapse.

Modulation Steps:
- Use Camel energy as a stabilising bridge
- Create rituals instead of rebellions
- Allow healing through consistency, not chaos

"Now my fire warms me. It doesn't consume me."

Common Shifts After Mastering Modulation

Emotional Health

- **Before**: Reactivity, self-blame, overwhelm

- ***After AMT Mastery***: Clarity, emotional pacing, reframing

Relationships

- **Before**: Overdependence, withdrawal, conflict
- ***After AMT Mastery***: Mutual understanding, flexible expression

Career

- **Before**: Stagnation, burnout, lack of purpose
- ***After AMT Mastery:*** Direction, adaptability, aligned success

Self-Worth

- **Before**: Identity confusion, shame, overthinking
- ***After AMT Mastery***: Embodiment, balance, confidence

❧

Your Story Is Still Unfolding

Every modulation story is different.
Some begin with shadow. Some with longing. Some with a deep ache to finally feel like themselves.

When you master modulation:
- You stop reacting
- You start responding
- You become a conductor of your own emotional orchestra

And most importantly —

You realise you were never broken.
Just unblended.

XXII

My Closing Letter to You

Dear Reader,

If you've reached this far, it means something inside you has shifted.
Maybe you've seen parts of yourself that were hidden.
Maybe you've started to forgive parts you once rejected.
Or maybe, for the first time, you feel like your emotional chaos finally has a structure.

Whatever it is — I want to honour it.
This letter isn't a conclusion. It's a beginning.

A Man on the Edge – The Case of "Vishal"

Vishal (name changed) was a 36-year-old architect. He came to me not with a diagnosis — but with a sentence:
"I've achieved everything I planned. But I hate waking up."

He wasn't depressed in the classic sense. He was successful, functional, respected. But his spark was missing.
His relationships were fraying. He described his state as a low-grade burn he couldn't locate.

Step 1: Identifying Possible Archetypes

Through emotional exploration, we saw fragments of:
- Eagle – clarity and visionary thinking
- Owl – constant analysis and withdrawal
- Tiger – push through stress aggressively
- Dolphin – memory of joy and ease

But none of these were central. Then came a revelation:
"I feel like I manipulate people emotionally, but I don't want to."

And there it was: Spider energy — in shadow.

Step 2: Understanding the Shadow – Cognitive Distortion

Spider's shadow involved:
- Control fallacy: "If I don't control people emotionally, I will be abandoned."
- Mind reading: "They're going to betray me. I must stay one step ahead."

His core belief: "To stay safe, I must always be two moves ahead. Even in love."

❧

Step 3: Confirming the Dominant Archetype

Despite multiple archetypes, Spider was dominant because:
- Emotional responses were driven by indirect influence
- He feared exposure more than failure
- He strategised even intimate moments

❧

Step 4: From Shadow to Bright

Golden Mean Reframe:
Trait: Strategy

- Shadow: Manipulation
- Golden Mean (Bright): Precision
- Excess: Rigid control

Trait: Communication

- Shadow: Cryptic
- Golden Mean (Bright): Transparent

- Excess: Passive-aggression

Trait: Emotion

- Shadow: Suppressed
- Golden Mean (Bright): Channelled
- Excess: Flatness

Reframed Belief: "I can influence outcomes without controlling people. Transparency is a strength — not a trap."

Step 5: Finding a Bridge Archetype

He couldn't access Dolphin or Dog directly.
Bridge used: Fox
- Shared cleverness with Spider
- Social adaptability of Dolphin

Modulation Practices:
- Speak truths playfully
- Use humour to access vulnerability
- Trust with boundaries

Step 6: Grounding the Change

Daily Tools:
- Morning: "What truth am I afraid to speak today?"

- Evening: "Where did strategy overpower sincerity?"
- Practice: One daily act of transparent communication

Results:
- Improved marriage warmth
- Greater social lightness
- Reconnection to creativity (abstract art)

Step 7: Identity Integration

- Spider became his tool, not his trap
- Fox helped unlock Dolphin
- He no longer hated waking up

From Me to You

You may be Vishal. Or someone completely different.

But within you are archetypes waiting to shift — not disappear.

Some are surviving. Some are hiding. Some are ready to lead.

Modulation is not perfection. It is permission — to learn, grow, blend.

You are not broken. You are flowable.

With love and faith in your inner animal world,

Dr. Nidheesh
Founder, Archetype Modulation Therapy

YOU ARE NOT AN ANIMAL — YOU ARE AN ENERGY IN MOTION

If there's one thing I hope this book made clear, it's this:

You are not a Lion, or a Rabbit, or a Snake.
You are not limited by fur, feather, claw, or symbol.

These archetypes are not boxes. They are currents — streams of energy I've witnessed move through thousands of lives. They're shapes your soul can borrow... just long enough to find itself again.

These animals? They're not your identity. They're your emotional language.

Through decades of work, I've seen these energies rise and fall like tides — some fierce, some fragile, some forgotten.

And this book? It only scratches the surface. There are many more archetypes still waiting to be mapped... minor flows, micro-patterns, silent shadows that still don't have names.
But you'll feel them. And when you do, don't ask "What animal am I?" Ask:

"What energy is speaking through me now?"

Use this book not as a label maker, but as a compass —
A gentle pointer that says: "You are here. You are feeling this. And you can move."

Like energy. Like light. Like life itself.

So go ahead — blend. Shift. Modulate. Fall apart, and form again.
You are allowed to change your shape without changing your soul.

That's not confusion. That's evolution.

And as always...
You are not broken. You are just becoming.

With deep respect,
Dr. Nidheesh

Appendix I

Trait Glossary

1 Adaptive

- Clever & Problem Solver
- Creative, Joyful, Healing
- Intelligent, Selective, Creative; Sensitive, Transformational
- Charming, Expressive
- Ability to flexibly respond to challenges using intellect, creativity, and emotional awareness, adjusting actions without losing core identity.
- Fox (2nd Degree); Dolphin (1st Degree); Cat (1st Degree); Frog (1st Degree); Butterfly (1st Degree)

2 Adaptiveness

- Creative, Joyful, Healing
- Intelligent, Selective, Creative
- Sensitive, Transformational
- Charming, Expressive
- Ability to adjust quickly to new conditions and solve problems with flexibility.
- Dolphin (1st Degree); Cat (1st Degree); Frog (1st Degree); Butterfly (1st Degree)

3 Agreeableness

- Wise, Empathetic, Responsible
- Creative, Joyful, Healing; Faithful, Companionable
- Insightful, Detached
- Disposition to be compassionate and cooperative toward others.
- Elephant (3rd Degree); Dolphin (1st Degree); Dog (1st Degree); Raven (1st Degree)

4 Conscientiousness

- Wise, Empathetic, Responsible
- Wise, Strategic, Deep Thinker
- Tendency to be organized, dependable, and disciplined.
- Elephant (3rd Degree); Owl (3rd Degree)

5 Control

- Patient, Creative Builder
- A tendency to regulate people, environments, or emotions in order to feel safe, often driven by fear of unpredictability or vulnerability.
- Spider (1st Degree)

6 Creativity

- Patient, Creative Builder; Charming, Expressive
- Capacity to generate original ideas, solutions, or artistic expressions.
- Spider (1st Degree); Butterfly (1st Degree)

&

7 Dark Triad

- Clever, Problem Solver
- A pattern of behaviours combining narcissism, Machiavellianism, and emotional coldness, often used to manipulate or dominate others.
- Fox (2nd Degree)

&

8 Dark Wisdom

- Insightful
- Detached Insight into the shadow aspects of human behaviour — including manipulation, pain, or power — used not to exploit, but to understand.
- Raven (1st Degree)

&

9 Deep Will

- Powerful, Regenerative
- Inner determination that remains focused through adversity, often emerging as resilience combined with a strong sense of purpose.

- Phoenix (3rd Degree)

છ

10 Dominance

- Fearless, Ambitious
- The assertive desire to lead or control, marked by a drive for authority, visibility, and goal enforcement.
- Tiger (1st Degree)

છ

11 Drive

- Bold, Assertive, Visionary; Fearless, Ambitious; Agile, Resourceful
- Motivation and ambition to pursue goals with persistence.
- Lion (3rd Degree); Tiger (1st Degree); Horse (1st Degree)

છ

12 Egoic Identity

- Charismatic, Expressive
- Self-perception driven by status, comparison, or image maintenance, often vulnerable to external approval or rejection.
- Peacock (2nd Degree)

છ

13 Emotional Depth

- Empathic, Stable
- Ability to feel, understand, and process deep emotional experiences.
- Whale (1ˢᵗ Degree)

14 Emotional Fluidity

- Creative, Joyful, Healing
- The capacity to shift emotional states smoothly and adaptively, allowing genuine expression without fixation.
- Dolphin (1ˢᵗ Degree)

15 Emotional Stability

Wise, Empathetic, Responsible

The ability to remain calm and regulated under stress, with minimal emotional reactivity and strong internal grounding.

Elephant (3ʳᵈ Degree)

16 Exploratory Creativity

- Charming, Expressive
- A desire to experiment with ideas, materials, or experiences in new ways, often driven by curiosity and play.

- Butterfly (1st Degree)

&

17 Expressive Ego

- Charismatic, Expressive
- A strong emotional presence that seeks to be seen and validated through dramatic, bold, or aesthetic self-presentation.
- Peacock (2nd Degree)

&

18 Extraversion

- Bold, Assertive, Visionary; Decisive, Alert, Precise; Charismatic, Expressive
- Orientation toward external stimulation, sociability, and assertiveness.
- Lion (3rd Degree); Hawk (1st Degree); Peacock (2nd Degree)

&

19 Focused Power

- Decisive, Alert, Precise
- The channelled use of strength, intellect, or emotion toward a precise target or purpose, often marked by discipline.
- Hawk (1st Degree)

&

20 **Freedom**

- Agile, Resourceful
- A psychological and behavioural preference for autonomy, choice, and movement without restriction or control.
- Horse (1st Degree)

&

21 **High Agreeableness**

- Creative, Joyful, Healing
- An enhanced tendency to cooperate, empathise, and maintain harmony in interpersonal situations, often at personal cost.
- Dolphin (1st Degree)

&

22 **High Energy**

- Fearless, Ambitious
- A state of sustained physical and emotional vitality, often experienced as enthusiasm, restlessness, or drive.
- Tiger (1st Degree)

&

23 **High Extraversion**

- Charismatic, Expressive

- Strong outward orientation toward social connection, stimulation, and action, with reduced need for solitude.
- Peacock (2nd Degree)

ॐ

24 High Neuroticism

- Alert, Adaptive
- Increased sensitivity to stress, negative feedback, and internal emotional conflict, often linked to mood instability.
- Rabbit (1st Degree)

ॐ

25 High Openness

- Creative, Joyful, Healing
- Intense receptivity to new ideas, emotions, experiences, and aesthetics, often linked to imagination and curiosity.
- Dolphin (1st Degree)

ॐ

26 Independence

- Intelligent, Selective, Creative
- The drive to make personal choices, solve problems alone, and define one's life without reliance on others.
- Cat (1st Degree)

෪

27 Independent Leadership

- Strategic, Broad Vision
- Ability to lead based on internal clarity and vision, often without requiring group validation or social consensus
- Eagle (3rd Degree)

෪

28 Inner Change

- Sensitive, Transformational
- Transformation that originates from emotional introspection or deep psychological shifts rather than external forces.
- Frog (1st Degree)

෪

29 Introspection

- Wise, Strategic, Deep Thinker
- Tendency toward inward-looking reflection and self-analysis.
- Owl (3rd Degree)

෪

30 Introverted Curiosity

- Intelligent, Selective, Creative

- Internal exploration of ideas, patterns, or meanings — often preferring silent observation over verbal interaction.
- Cat (1st Degree)

ॐ

31 Introverted Leadership

- Team-Driven, Loyal, Observant
- Leading quietly through example, observation, or mentorship, often driven by consistency and integrity over charisma.
- Wolf (2nd Degree)

ॐ

32 Intuitive Flexibility

- Intelligent, Selective, Creative
- Fluid adaptation based on internal perception of what feels emotionally or energetically aligned, not just logical.
- Cat (1st Degree)

ॐ

33 Leadership

- Bold, Assertive, Visionary
- Team-Driven, Loyal, Observant
- Strategic, Broad Vision
- Powerful, Regenerative

- Ability to guide, influence, and inspire others effectively.
- Lion (3rd Degree); Wolf (2nd Degree); Eagle (3rd Degree); Phoenix (3rd Degree)

&

34 **Lightness**

- Charming, Expressive
- An energetic quality of ease, joy, or humour that uplifts situations or people without being superficial.
- Butterfly (1st Degree)

&

35 **Low Agreeableness**

- Insightful, Detached
- A tendency to prioritise personal truth or autonomy over interpersonal harmony, often perceived as assertive or cold.
- Raven (1st Degree)

&

36 **Low Openness**

- Grounded, Protective, Reliable; Disciplined, Long-Term Focus
- Preference for familiarity, order, and tradition, with reduced comfort toward ambiguity or novelty.
- Bear (1st Degree); Camel (1st Degree)

ॐ

37 Loyal Support

- Faithful, Companionable
- Emotional dedication to others, marked by reliability, empathy, and presence, especially in times of need.
- Dog (1st Degree)

ॐ

38 Loyalty

- Team-Driven, Loyal, Observant; Faithful, Companionable
- Faithfulness or devotion to people, duties, or values.
- Wolf (2nd Degree); Dog (1st Degree)

ॐ

39 Machiavellian

- Calculative, Controlled
- Skilled manipulation and strategic control of others for personal gain.
- Snake (1st Degree)

ॐ

40 Movement

- Agile, Resourceful
- A physical and psychological drive toward progress,

travel, or change, often resisting confinement or stillness
- Horse (1st Degree)

41 **Neuroticism**

- Sensitive, Transformational; Alert, Adaptive
- Tendency to experience intense emotional fluctuations, worry, and vulnerability to psychological stress
- Frog (1st Degree); Rabbit (1st Degree)

42 **Nurturance**

- Wise, Empathetic, Responsible; Empathic, Stable
- A deep emotional drive to care for, protect, and support others in a sensitive and consistent manner.
- Elephant (3rd Degree); Whale (1st Degree)

43 **Observer**

- Insightful, Detached
- A perceptive stance of watching, understanding, and reflecting rather than immediately acting or speaking.
- Raven (1st Degree)

44 Openness

- Grounded, Protective, Reliable; Wise, Strategic, Deep Thinker; Creative, Joyful, Healing; Disciplined, Long-Term Focus
- Willingness to engage with new experiences, ideas, and emotions.
- Bear (1st Degree); Owl (3rd Degree); Dolphin (1st Degree); Camel (1st Degree)

&

45 Opportunistic

- Clever, Problem Solver
- The ability to recognise and act on chances for gain or advantage, often using strategic timing or subtle influence.
- Fox (2nd Degree)

&

46 Patience

- Patient
- The emotional capacity to wait, endure, or build slowly without frustration, often rooted in long-term vision.
- Spider (1st Degree)

&

47 Planning

- Creative Builder
- The structured ability to forecast, organise, and prepare sequential actions to meet goals efficiently.
- Spider (1st Degree)

48 Practical Drive

- Agile, Resourceful
- Motivation to pursue realistic, action-based solutions, often focused on effectiveness over idealism.
- Horse (1st Degree)

49 Precision

- Patient, Creative Builder
- Attention to fine detail and accuracy, both mentally and behaviourally, often tied to perfectionistic tendencies.
- Spider (1st Degree)

50 Rebirth

- Powerful, Regenerative
- A process of internal transformation where old patterns are shed and new strengths emerge, often after crisis.
- Phoenix (3rd Degree)

51 **Resilience**

- Disciplined, Long-Term Focus; Powerful, Regenerative
- Capacity to recover quickly from adversity or setbacks.
- Camel (1st Degree); Phoenix (3rd Degree)

&

52 **Self-preserving**

- Calculative, Controlled
- Behaviours motivated by safety, control, and protection of emotional or physical vulnerability.
- Snake (1st Degree)

&

53 **Sensitivity**

- Sensitive, Transformational; Alert, Adaptive
- Responsiveness to emotional, environmental, or interpersonal stimuli.
- Frog (1st Degree); Rabbit (1st Degree)

&

54 **Silent Wisdom**

- Empathic, Stable
- Subtle, intuitive knowledge expressed through presence, timing, or quiet support rather than verbal explanation.
- Whale (1st Degree)

৯

55 **Social Charisma**

- Charismatic, Expressive
- A magnetic presence in social situations, combining confidence, expressiveness, and emotional intelligence.
- Peacock (2nd Degree)

৯

56 **Social Curiosity**

- Charming
- Expressive Interest in understanding people, dynamics, and social trends, often through interaction or observation.
- Butterfly (1st Degree)

৯

57 **Social Harmony**

- Faithful, Companionable
- An emotional skill of creating peace, reducing conflict, and tuning behaviour for relational balance.
- Dog (1st Degree)

৯

58 **Stability**

- Grounded, Protective, Reliable; Wise, Empathetic,

Responsible

- A sense of internal calm, predictability, and regulation that resists being thrown off by external chaos.
- Bear (1st Degree); Elephant (3rd Degree)

ଛ

59 **Strategic**

- Calculative, Controlled
- Oriented toward long-term outcomes and optimisation, often using foresight and subtle manipulation.
- Snake (1st Degree)

ଛ

60 **Strategy**

- Team-Driven, Loyal, Observant
- Capacity to plan and execute long-term actions to achieve goals.
- Wolf (2nd Degree)

ଛ

61 **Strength**

- Grounded, Protective, Reliable
- Core ability to remain firm, grounded, and enduring under stress.
- Bear (1st Degree)

ଛ

62 Subtle Control

- Patient, Creative Builder Influence applied without overt force — through tone, silence, timing, or emotional calibration. Spider (1st Degree)

ॐ

63 Transformation

- Sensitive, Transformational; Powerful, Regenerative
- Deep structural change of self, identity, or belief patterns, often arising from emotional breakthrough.
- Frog (1st Degree); Phoenix (3rd Degree)

ॐ

64 Transformational Leadership

- Powerful, Regenerative
- The ability to inspire significant change in others by modelling growth, courage, and emotional authenticity
- Phoenix (3rd Degree)

ॐ

65 Transformational Sensitivity

- Sensitive, Transformational
- A heightened emotional openness that, when processed consciously, becomes the root of profound change.
- Frog (1st Degree)

ॐ

66 Visionary Strategic, Broad Vision

- An intuitive, imaginative foresight that sees future possibilities and builds toward them with clarity.
- Eagle (3rd Degree)

ॐ

67 Wise Nurturance

- Wise, Empathetic, Responsible
- Support that combines empathy with discernment, giving care without overextending or enabling.
- Elephant (3rd Degree)

Major and Minor Archetypes – Classification & Core Feature

This appendix provides a classification of AMT archetypes into Major and Minor categories. Each archetype is listed with its core emotional or behavioural feature that defines its influence. Major archetypes represent dominant emotional lenses capable of shaping identity independently, while Minor archetypes usually express in supportive or context-dependent ways.

Archetype Classification – Core Feature List

Major Archetypes

- Lion – Courageous Leadership
- Elephant – Stable Empathy and Wisdom
- Owl – Strategic Insight and Reflection
- Snake – Survival Instinct with Emotional Calculation
- Dolphin – Joyful Healing and Social Flow
- Dog – Loyal Support and Connection
- Whale – Emotional Depth and Silence
- Phoenix – Transformational Rebirth
- Tiger – Raw Drive and Dominance
- Spider – Precision and Emotional Strategy
- Eagle – Visionary Clarity and Elevation
- Wolf – Pack Loyalty and Intuitive Leadership

- Bear – Grounded Strength and Protection

Minor Archetypes

- Fox – Adaptive Cleverness
- Cat – Introspective Independence
- Peacock – Charisma and Aesthetic Expression
- Frog – Emotional Sensitivity During Transition
- Rabbit – Hypervigilant Alertness and Vulnerability
- Horse – Momentum and Freedom
- Butterfly – Lightness and Creativity
- Camel – Endurance and Minimalism
- Raven – Symbolic Intelligence and Shadow Insight
- Hawk – Focused Targeting and Observation

Archetype Modulation Map – From Shadow to Bright

This appendix provides a structured modulation map for each archetype, guiding practitioners from the Shadow expression to the Bright state using the Golden Mean. Each entry includes compatible archetypes, suggested bridge archetypes for indirect modulation, and practical cues for transitioning states.

Lion

- Shadow State: Aggressive, dominating, attention-seeking
- Golden Mean: Calm authority and constructive confidence
- Bright Expression: Assertive leader who empowers others
- Compatible Archetypes: Dog, Owl, Eagle
- Bridge Archetypes: Tiger

Rabbit

- Shadow State: Hypervigilant, anxious, avoids attention
- Golden Mean: Sensitive awareness with inner safety
- Bright Expression: Alert, gentle, emotionally attuned
- Compatible Archetypes: Dolphin, Dog
- Bridge Archetypes: Fox, Cat

Phoenix

- Shadow State: Self-destructive transformation, intense volatility
- Golden Mean: Controlled renewal with conscious intention
- Bright Expression: Rebirth and healing through deliberate change
- Compatible Archetypes: Frog, Raven
- Bridge Archetypes: Whale

Spider

- Shadow State: Emotionally manipulative, overly strategic
- Golden Mean: Subtle influence with transparency
- Bright Expression: Patient planner with emotional control
- Compatible Archetypes: Fox, Owl
- Bridge Archetypes: Dolphin

Butterfly

- Shadow State: Escapist, lacks roots, emotional inconsistency
- Golden Mean: Creative lightness grounded in presence
- Bright Expression: Playful, artistic, emotionally fluid
- Compatible Archetypes: Dolphin, Horse
- Bridge Archetypes: Cat

Bear

- Shadow State: Overprotective, rigid, emotionally

withdrawn
- Golden Mean: Firm yet flexible emotional presence
- Bright Expression: Grounded, nurturing, protective strength
- Compatible Archetypes: Elephant, Camel
- Bridge Archetypes: Phoenix

Elephant

- Shadow State: Overburdened, emotionally enmeshed
- Golden Mean: Empathic structure and healthy detachment
- Bright Expression: Wise, grounded, emotionally strong presence
- Compatible Archetypes: Whale, Bear
- Bridge Archetypes: Camel

Owl

- Shadow State: Detached, overthinking, emotionally cold
- Golden Mean: Analytical with emotional integration
- Bright Expression: Insightful, calm, emotionally aware
- Compatible Archetypes: Eagle, Spider
- Bridge Archetypes: Dolphin

Fox

- Shadow State: Cunning, evasive, emotionally avoidant
- Golden Mean: Adaptability with honesty
- Bright Expression: Tactful, quick-witted, emotionally smart
- Compatible Archetypes: Cat, Snake
- Bridge Archetypes: Rabbit

Snake

- Shadow State: Paranoid, secretive, controlling
- Golden Mean: Cautious intuition with relational clarity
- Bright Expression: Protective strategist with emotional restraint
- Compatible Archetypes: Owl, Spider
- Bridge Archetypes: Fox

Dolphin

- Shadow State: Overaccommodating, avoids conflict, performative joy
- Golden Mean: Genuine joy with honest emotion
- Bright Expression: Expressive, light-hearted, socially healing
- Compatible Archetypes: Rabbit, Butterfly
- Bridge Archetypes: Cat

Cat

- Shadow State: Withdrawn, dismissive, hyper-independent
- Golden Mean: Self-sufficient with openness
- Bright Expression: Graceful, intuitive, emotionally poised
- Compatible Archetypes: Fox, Owl
- Bridge Archetypes: Dog

Dog

- Shadow State: Over-loyal, co-dependent, suppresses needs

- Golden Mean: Supportive with boundaries
- Bright Expression: Warm, grounded, emotionally consistent
- Compatible Archetypes: Lion, Rabbit
- Bridge Archetypes: Elephant

Peacock

- Shadow State: Image-obsessed, performative, validation-seeking
- Golden Mean: Authentic self-expression
- Bright Expression: Confident, radiant, expressive from truth
- Compatible Archetypes: Butterfly, Dolphin
- Bridge Archetypes: Horse

Whale

- Shadow State: Overwhelmed, silently suffering, avoids expression
- Golden Mean: Emotional richness with containment
- Bright Expression: Deep, nurturing, powerfully silent
- Compatible Archetypes: Elephant, Raven
- Bridge Archetypes: Phoenix

Frog

- Shadow State: Emotionally unstable, stuck in cycles of uncertainty
- Golden Mean: Transitional insight with self-trust
- Bright Expression: Emotionally aware, evolving gracefully
- Compatible Archetypes: Whale, Phoenix

- Bridge Archetypes: Rabbit

Tiger

- Shadow State: Explosive, confrontational, unrestrained drive
- Golden Mean: Focused ambition with emotional balance
- Bright Expression: Dynamic, courageous, inspiring energy
- Compatible Archetypes: Lion, Horse
- Bridge Archetypes: Owl

Horse

- Shadow State: Avoids commitment, overvalues freedom
- Golden Mean: Free with focused will
- Bright Expression: Agile, independent, purpose-driven
- Compatible Archetypes: Butterfly, Hawk
- Bridge Archetypes: Camel

Eagle

- Shadow State: Aloof, overly critical, disconnected from emotion
- Golden Mean: High-level vision with heart
- Bright Expression: Focused, discerning, emotionally clear
- Compatible Archetypes: Owl, Hawk
- Bridge Archetypes: Whale

Camel

- Shadow State: Emotionally dry, avoids connection,

overly self-contained

- Golden Mean: Sustainable endurance with emotional rhythm
- Bright Expression: Simple, emotionally regulated, supportive
- Compatible Archetypes: Bear, Elephant
- Bridge Archetypes: Owl

Raven

- Shadow State: Darkly withdrawn, cryptic, symbolically stuck
- Golden Mean: Symbolic intelligence with vulnerability
- Bright Expression: Reflective, intuitive, translator of shadow
- Compatible Archetypes: Whale, Phoenix
- Bridge Archetypes: Owl

Wolf

- Shadow State: Tribal, aggressive, fear-based loyalty
- Golden Mean: Protective collaboration with inner intuition
- Bright Expression: Bonded, balanced, leads with presence
- Compatible Archetypes: Dog, Bear
- Bridge Archetypes: Elephant

Hawk

- Shadow State: Hyper-focused, rigid, emotionally suppressive
- Golden Mean: Focused clarity with adaptive range
- Bright Expression: Strategic, emotionally composed, driven
- Compatible Archetypes: Eagle, Horse
- Bridge Archetypes: Fox

Appendix IV

Modulation Hints Guide – Behavioural Cues for Archetypal Balance

This appendix outlines clear, actionable behaviours that support or disrupt each archetype. For each archetype, you'll find:
- **DO**: Habits that enhance the archetype's bright expression
- **DON'T**: Habits that can distort or suppress the energy
- **WARNING**: Specific archetypal patterns to avoid adopting due to incompatibility

Lion

DO (Enhancing Habits)
- Speak with calm authority
- Delegate and inspire
- Lead by example in pressure

DON'T (Distorting Habits)
- Yell to gain control
- Disregard team input
- Seek validation via dominance

Warning: Avoid habits of Peacock, Bear

Elephant

DO
· Journal wise reflections
· Hold space for others' emotions
· Share one structured insight daily
DON'T
· Absorb others' pain silently
· Avoid vulnerability
· Become stoic out of fear
Warning: Tiger, Cat

Owl

DO
· Reflect before reacting
· Write observations instead of judgments
· Guide others subtly
DON'T
· Over-analyse feelings
· Withhold emotion as weakness
· Judge without empathy
Warning: Tiger, Butterfly

Fox

DO
· Reframe problems creatively

- Use humour to resolve tension
- Shift social gears wisely
    DON'T
- Lie to maintain control
- Manipulate subtly for self-gain
    Warning: Dog, Phoenix

Snake

DO
- Observe without paranoia
- Protect emotional space with honesty
- Set silent boundaries
    DON'T
- Assume betrayal by default
- Emotionally corner others
    Warning: Dolphin, Rabbit

Dolphin

DO
- Laugh openly with others
- Compliment sincerely
- Share struggles gently
    DON'T
- Hide sadness behind jokes
- Please others to avoid conflict
    Warning: Snake, Spider

Cat

DO
- Spend quiet time daily
- Express needs without guilt
- Enjoy solitude as a resource

DON'T
- Ghost people to punish
- Push others away after bonding

Warning: Dog, Peacock

Dog

DO
- Check in emotionally with loved ones
- Support without overextending
- Celebrate loyalty openly

DON'T
- Depend excessively on approval
- Hide your own feelings to keep peace

Warning: Snake, Cat

Peacock

DO
- Express your story with truth
- Dress creatively for yourself

- Compliment others genuinely
    DON'T
- Brag to gain applause
- Use charm to cover insecurity
    Warning: Camel, Owl

ಣ

Whale

DO
- Spend time in silence
- Write feelings in metaphors
- Rest deeply when overwhelmed
    DON'T
- Suppress pain entirely
- Isolate without expression
    Warning: Lion, Tiger

ಣ

Phoenix

DO
- Use a ritual for closure (burn paper, bury object)
- Start new projects after reflection
- Express grief safely
    DON'T
- Burn bridges emotionally
- Create chaos to feel 'alive'
    Warning: Bear, Horse

ಣ

Frog

DO
- Track emotions in phases (e.g., moon cycle)
- Journal emotional shifts daily
- Allow silent transitions
    DON'T
- Rush change without clarity
- Get stuck in indecision
    Warning: Tiger, Eagle

∞

Rabbit

DO
- Keep a consistent daily rhythm
- Ground with breath when anxious
- Stay in soft lighting or quiet space
    DON'T
- Overexpose to stimuli
- Avoid social safety altogether
    Warning: Tiger, Spider

∞

Tiger

DO
- Lift weights or run
- Set one major goal per week
- Channel energy in creative fight

DON'T
- React with violence
- Bulldoze others' boundaries
	Warning: Rabbit, Whale

Horse

DO
- Take solo nature walks
- Say 'no' with love
- Schedule open time blocks
	DON'T
- Flee commitment out of fear
- Detach when intimacy increases
	Warning: Bear, Phoenix

Butterfly

DO
- Try a new colour daily
- Keep a dream sketchbook
- Compliment someone creatively
	DON'T
- Flit between people for approval
- Avoid endings altogether
	Warning: Camel, Elephant

Spider

DO
- Map your emotional plan weekly
- Use silence as power
- Delay response until ready
    DON'T
- Test loyalty secretly
- Influence through guilt
    Warning: Dolphin, Rabbit

Eagle

DO
- Set long-term vision board
- Meditate for mental clarity
- Review goals monthly
    DON'T
- Isolate in superiority
- Criticise to feel powerful
    Warning: Peacock, Frog

Camel

DO
- Fast from digital distractions
- Maintain basic routines
- Say little, mean more

DON'T
- Suppress joy entirely
- Withhold all emotion
     Warning: Butterfly, Peacock

&

Raven

DO
- Study symbolism (e.g., Tarot, myth)
- Reflect on dreams weekly
- Speak one hard truth softly
     DON'T
- Live in riddles
- Avoid direct answers always
     Warning: Lion, Tiger

&

Wolf

DO
- Organise community tasks
- Sit in circle discussions
- Lead through silent presence
     DON'T
- Police everyone emotionally
- Attack when excluded
     Warning: Peacock, Cat

&

Hawk

DO
- Use to-do lists daily
- Focus on one mission at a time
- Practice zoom-out reflection
  DON'T
- Micromanage others
- Obsess over perfection
  Warning: Rabbit, Whale

Bear

DO
- Carry responsibility lightly
- Use your hands to create (craft, garden)
- Rest like it's sacred
  DON'T
- Refuse to change for anyone
- Hold grudges silently
  Warning: Phoenix, Peacock

Cognitive Distortions – A Guide to Shadow Thinking

Cognitive distortions are automatic, inaccurate patterns of thought that reinforce negative emotions and behaviours. In AMT, these distortions often reflect a shadow state of an archetype.

Understanding them is the first step toward modulating into clarity.

∞

1. All-or-Nothing Thinking (Black-and-White Thinking)

Definition: Seeing things in extremes — as all good or all bad, perfect or a failure.
Example: "If I don't succeed in this presentation, I'm worthless."
Archetypal Shadow: Hawk, Eagle

∞

2. Overgeneralisation

Definition: Making sweeping conclusions based on a single event or pattern.
Example: "I failed once, I always fail."
Archetypal Shadow: Rabbit, Frog

ॐ

3. Mental Filtering

Definition: Focusing only on the negatives, ignoring the positives.
Example: "They complimented me, but mentioned one flaw — so I clearly failed."
Archetypal Shadow: Owl, Whale

ॐ

4. Disqualifying the Positive

Definition: Dismissing genuine positive experiences or feedback.
Example: "They said I did well, but they were just being polite."
Archetypal Shadow: Rabbit, Peacock

ॐ

5. Jumping to Conclusions

Mind Reading: Assuming others' thoughts or intentions.
Example: "She didn't reply because she hates me."
Fortune Telling: Predicting negative outcomes without proof.
Example: "There's no point applying — I'll never get it."
Archetypal Shadow: Snake, Fox, Raven

ॐ

6. Catastrophising

Definition: Expecting the worst-case scenario and blowing problems out of proportion.
Example: "If I make a mistake, everything will collapse."
Archetypal Shadow: Rabbit, Phoenix

7. Emotional Reasoning

Definition: Believing something must be true because it "feels" that way.
Example: "I feel anxious, so something bad must be about to happen."
Archetypal Shadow: Frog, Dolphin

8. Should Statements

Definition: Rigid internal rules that create guilt or frustration.
Example: "I should never feel tired." / "They should respect me."
Archetypal Shadow: Bear, Lion

9. Labelling and Mislabelling

Definition: Defining yourself or others with a single, negative word.
Example: "I'm a loser." / "He's a failure."
Archetypal Shadow: Tiger, Camel

10. Personalisation

Definition: Blaming yourself for things outside your control.
Example: "My friend is upset — it must be because of something I did."
Archetypal Shadow: Dog, Whale

11. Blame Shifting

Definition: Attributing responsibility entirely to others instead of self-reflection.
Example: "This didn't work because of them, not me."
Archetypal Shadow: Lion, Spider

12. Magnification and Minimisation

Definition: Exaggerating flaws or shrinking achievements.
Example: "One typo ruined the whole report." / "It wasn't a big deal that I helped."
Archetypal Shadow: Peacock, Cat

13. Control Fallacies

External Control: Believing your life is entirely dictated by others.
Example: "I can't be happy unless they approve."
Internal Control: Believing you're responsible for everyone's feelings.
Example: "It's my fault they're upset."
Archetypal Shadow: Dog, Elephant, Snake

14. Fallacy of Fairness

Definition: Believing life must be fair and feeling wronged when it's not.
Example: "It's unfair that I work harder but get less recognition."
Archetypal Shadow: Wolf, Raven

15. Heaven's Reward Fallacy

Definition: Believing hard work guarantees external reward — and feeling bitter when it doesn't.
Example: "After all I've done, I deserve better."
Archetypal Shadow: Bear, Camel

16. Imposter Syndrome (Related)

Definition: Feeling like a fraud despite real accomplishments.
Example: "I just got lucky — I don't belong here."
Archetypal Shadow: Peacock, Rabbit

> "*Each of these distortions is a window into shadow energy.*
> *When identified, they can be transformed — reframed through the Golden Mean of each archetype and consciously modulated.*"

A Thought To Conclude ....

"You are not here to be labelled.
You are here to learn your rhythm, your
energy, your light.
And when you learn to shift, blend, and
rise —
you become the healer you were always
searching for."

— Dr. P. Nidheesh, MD (Hom)

* 9 7 9 8 8 9 9 0 6 8 6 7 6 *